ISBN 978-1-330-44344-6
PIBN 10062974

FB &c Ltd, Dalton House, 60 Windsor Avenue, London, SW19 2RR.
Company number 08720141. Registered in England and Wales.

For support please visit www.forgottenbooks.com

MASANIELLO

AND OTHER POEMS

BY

HENRY LOCKWOOD

AUTHOR OF "SACRED LYRICS," "AXEL," ETC. ETC.

LONDON:

KERBY & ENDEAN, 440 OXFORD STREET

1883.

PREFACE.

IN offering this small collection to the reader, it is felt that some words of apology may be requisite for the unfinished condition of the poem which gives its name to the volume. The Editor can only state in explanation, that the work was cut short by the sudden death of its much lamented author, and she feels sure that this circumstance—while investing it with an additional, if painful, interest to personal friends—will ensure the indulgence of the general reader.

The succession of the pieces, however, is the same as was intended had the interstices been filled up, and will, it is thought, suffice to give the leading ideas of the poem.

BOURNEMOUTH, *December* 1882.

CONTENTS.

TRANSLATIONS.

MASANIELLO.

AN UNFINISHED POËM.

Masañiello (Tommaso Aniello) a fisherman of Naples, was born at Amalfi, 1623. He was the chief promoter and leader of the revolt of the Neapolitan people in 1647 against the grinding tyranny of the Spanish Viceroy, the Duke of Arcos, who had brought the exasperation of the populace to a climax by the heavy taxation of their principal articles of food. Masaniello, young, handsome, and very popular in his own class, fired with the thought of delivering his countrymen from the yoke of the oppressor, and also of avenging the unjust imprisonment of his young wife, put himself at the head of the insurgents, who were ready to obey his slightest word. Under his orders, they broke into and rifled the palace, in spite of the resistance of the guards, and, the Viceroy having fled, they proclaimed their idol Captain of the People and sole Ruler of Naples. After a few days, however, the excitement of brain caused by these events, produced in Masaniello fits of frenzy or insanity, by some attributed to poison. During these, he was guilty of many acts of tyrannical cruelty and even of massacres, which quickly alienated his followers. The result was that, on the tenth day after his sudden elevation, he was treacherously assassinated in the convent to which he had retired for safety.

MASANIELLO.

"FAR—far as the billows of ocean can roam,
"To the confines of earth be found Liberty's home;
"No limits for ever be set to her reign;
"O'er Italy's shore may her star never wane!

"When the wrath of the Tyrant our homes shall assail,
"And his hirelings descend over mountain and vale,
"May the Angel of Death mow their ranks on the field,
"And Victory's laurels encircle our shield!

"Yea! the just God of battles will list to our cry,
"For the sighs of the mourner are echoed on high;
"The dayspring must rise on our night of despair,
"As the tempest is hushed by the spirits of air.

"With the speed of the breakers that whiten the
bay,
"Let us marshal our forces in battle array,
"Give for kindred and hearth the last drop of our
blood,
"And fall on the foe with the strength of a flood.

"Then the voice of our sorrow and anguish shall
cease,
"As the war-cloud is chased by the sunshine of peace;
"And the standard of Freedom for ever shall wave
"O'er the brows of the Free, in the hands of the
Brave!"

Across that quiet sheltered bay,
Whose waters flash the sapphire's ray
And kiss the feet of Capri's isle,
Whereon the skies e'er seem to smile,
These stirring stanzas rose and fell
In cadence clear,—a magic spell
To flush the cheek and light the eye
With fire that claims its birth on high,
And move the soul to mightiest deed
For which a patriot fain would bleed.

And on those forms that lined the shore,
Whose accents drowned the ocean's roar,
The moon shed pale uncertain rays
Like distant gleams of happier days,—
Lit with her soft mysterious light
The mountain's crest and Capri's height,—

O'er the vined plains deep shadows threw,
And bathed the waves in silvery hue,—
Now gleamed with radiant floods of light,
Now veiled her rays in darkest night,—
Type of man's fortune here below :
A shifting scene of joy and woe.

And who those men whose wrath would vie
With thunder crashing o'er the sky?
Their flashing eyes and knitted brows
Foretell they came not to carouse;
If other signs were wanting still
To prove their presence augurs ill
To some oppressor's galling chain
E'er e'en perchance yon moon should wane,
The close-set lips, the livid cheek,
And the clenched hand full well bespeak

That foulest wrongs and darkest deeds
In patriot breasts have sown their seeds.

Ere the last notes had died away
Borne by the breeze across the bay,
Swift rushing breakers wreathed the sands
With brightly gleaming silver bands,
Till ocean's furrowed cheek grew pale
Before the might of the rising gale;
And o'er the mountain's jagged crest,
Where night's still shadow seemed to rest,
The lightning shed a ghastly glow
Like hues of death on face of woe,
And earth the mirror of anger seemed,
That on the brow of Heaven gleamed.

From hill to hill, from vale to vale,
Above the roar of tempest's wail,
O'er the lashed waters deepest hold,
In ceaseless peals the thunder rolled ;
And fiery shafts were hurled around
Till quivering boughs obscured the ground,
'Neath shattered trunks of shapeless form,
The blackened harvest of the storm ;
While shrillest shrieks of birds of prey
Lent discord to that savage fray,
That wildly raged o'er earth and sky
As if God's trump were heard on high.

* *

The watch is set, the beacon gleams,
And on each swarthy face there beams
A glowing, weird, uncertain light,
As meteors shed through mists of night.
Muffled in cloaks, their couch the ground,
Pillowed on rocks that lie around,
They seek an hour's brief repose
Ere the chief bids them meet their foes;
Perchance to dream their bonds cut free
By the bright sword of liberty;
And he their Chief, Dictator, King,
For whom the shouts so fiercely ring
From Naples' sunny sheltered bay
To Ischia's steepest rugged way,
From Pæstum's plain and Capri's isle
To where Amalfi's headlands smile!

But who that Chief so firmly throned
In hearts by wildest impulse owned,—
Who knew no law save Passion's strife,
No rule to guide a wayward life,
But fickle as his changing clime
Now clung to virtue, now to crime?
Unblessed by wealth and lowly born,
He'd early learnt the rich to scorn
As scorpions who, with deadly sting,
The cruel shaft of poison wing;
And his pulse throbbed the chains to part
That coiled around his country's heart.
He saw the mother's glistening tear,
The blanching cheek, the gaze of fear,
The anxious start at every sound
That might reveal the menial's round
To wrest the crust so hardly won

From earliest morn to setting sun.
By many a cottage porch he saw
The gathered vultures of the law
Seizing, as if their hearts were stone,
The last the peasant called his own ;
And this a tyrant's greed to sate
Blinded with love of pomp and state.
All this he saw, and cursed the hour
That dawned upon that tyrant's power.
Oft when he mingled in the dance,
Mirrored in some dark beauty's glance,
Unmindful of those orbs of light
Sparkling like starry gems at night,
His thoughts would wander far away,
As if he spurned their softest ray ;
The thrilling pressure, sunny smile
Playing on lips that seemed the while

To echo notes from Heaven above,
All the mute eloquence of Love,
That mighty lord of kings and slaves,—
The golden sceptre beauty waves,—
Howe'er, how oft these might essay,—
Could not o'er *him* assert their sway;
But, as the phantoms of a dream
When light and reason once more beam,
They left no trace, no sign to tell
Of efforts wrought to work their spell.
As misers weigh a trifle's cost,
He deemed each precious moment lost,
Spent in the gay and giddy throng
'Mid dance and music, jest and song;
And sought escape from human gaze
In Nature's hidden, silent ways,
Where brooding o'er his country's woes

He vowed revenge on all her foes.
While with such thoughts his brain was rife
He chose a fisher's hardy life,
Free as the breeze he loved to court,
Unfettered as the billow's sport
O'er ocean's wide and pathless realm,
Thro' which he fearless guides his helm,
And nerves his arm and learns his pow'r
To smile at danger's darkest hour.

All of resolve and force of mind
That in man's soul were e'er enshrined,—
A strength to crush an iron will
By every art those gifts instil,
To bend men like the pliant steel,
And teach them all that strength to feel,—
Such arms were his,—and his to prize

More than all others 'neath the skies,—
Till patriot bands from near and far
Were pledged to freedom's holy war.
Thus had he watched from bud to bloom,
Thro' sunshine hours and days of gloom,
And many a dreaded trial past,
The blossom yield its fruit at last,
And Liberty with strong mailed hand
Sow her first seed throughout the land.

*

And now the moon, as in past halcyon days,
Sheds the full splendour of her glorious rays,
Floods the broad heavens with a dazzling sheen,
And o'er the waters sits enthroned as Queen,—
Athwart each rock her silvery mantle throws,

While every leaf with slender fret-work glows,
And thro' the vale mysterious shadows rise
Like spirits lingering 'neath the midnight skies.
Save for the sentry's firmly measured tread,
The slumbering camp seems like a field of dead,
Whereo'er the moonbeams, girt with fleecy clouds,
Weave in the stillness their transparent shrouds.
Led by the star of distant beacon's light,
Like glow-worm glistening in the summer night,
Through the lone valley Masaniello strode,
By motives urged that heroes onward goad,
Whate'er the shoals that bar their stormy way
Till the morn heralds a more hopeful day.—
His bourne was reached,—the password asked and
said,—
The outpost questioned and the orders read,—
The signal given that the Chief is there

The camp to cheer and all their hopes to share.
A smile—a nod—a grasp for every hand—
Thus Masaniello ever met his band;
And in that greeting was unbared the heart,
The love that nought but death alone could part.
But as he neared the torches burning low,
And on his brow there shone a sudden glow,
They marked depression's dark unwonted seal
That some disaster might too soon reveal.
Whate'er he felt, his eye, ne'er taught to quail,
Surveyed them calmly as he told his tale,—
The web unravelled of those meshes spread
By Intrigue's hand to crush Rebellion's head,
The hidden perils that their cause assailed,
Before whose depths all other dangers paled,—
And counselled caution, subtle, ripened schemes,
Thoughts well matured, not evanescent dreams;

And then by gradual, faintly traced degrees,
That keenest minds are often slow to seize,
He changed his tone, and firmly took his stand
On higher ground, to gain, enforce command.
He spoke as leader, with uplifted arm
Weighting his words, to bid them swift disarm,
Till some more genial and auspicious hour
Proclaimed the morn of their resistless pow'r.

Deep were the murmurs, loud the curses breathed,
Carbines unslung and poniards fast unsheathed,
Hands raised to Heav'n with fierce unconscious grace,
Brows tightly knit and scowls on every face.
Clear signs were there that e'en their Leader's blood
Might slake the fury of that human flood,
That seemed to rage 'neath disappointment's blow
Fiercely as breakers o'er their barriers flow.

Unmoved he stood amid that maddened band,
Scarce touched his weapon with a careless hand;
But scans in silence and with saddened eyes
The forms that round him wildly surge and rise.
For well he knew that in those Southern veins
A fevered current oft an entrance gains,
To cool before the power enthroned above
And lent to man,—the potent charm of love.
No vain belief,—for, as in springtide days
The clouds are chased by sunshine's cheering rays,
They felt their love in all its strength return,
Fresh forces gather, with fresh ardour burn,
Till 'mid the *vivas* for his future fame
They mingled blessings on their Captain's name!

* * * * *

There is a passion sways the human breast,
An ever present, tho' unbidden guest,
Whose subtle fire every heart must feel,—
Pure, strong, unchanging, stamp'd with Heaven's
seal
When most 'tis felt, as God Himself designed,—
The hallowed link that should enchain mankind;
No rage nor clime can quench this mystic flame,
The noblest title and the lowliest name
Must bend before the universal shrine,
Adore, confess it springs from source divine,
And shall endure till Earth has passed away,
And night is changed into eternal day.

It was the eve's soft twilight hour,
When dew-drops gem the drooping flow'r,
And trees in darker vesture stand

Like phantoms in a fairy land,
When silence steals o'er vale and hill
And even Nature's heart seems still;
While floating in a sea of gold
The clouds their opal hues unfold
To tint the pure transparent sky
And pass away like Summer's sigh,—
Ere yet the silvery crescent's light
Glistens on the brow of night,
Or the first planet sheds her ray
To gladden the departing day.

Another sun on Earth had set;
Another day of toil was o'er;
Dark passions had in tumult met
Once more by Ischia's silent shore.
And Masaniello paced the strand,

While rippling waves their music breathed
To pebbles on the golden sand
With Ocean's sapphire chaplet wreathed.
Those echoes mocked his restless life,
The deeds with which his brain o'erflowed :
They spoke of peace, *he* thought of strife
And death, the debt to Tyrants owed.

But hark! The Tarantella's dance
Wafts its loved music to the shore,
And sweetest smile and brightest glance
O'er many a heart in triumph soar.
As parched earth smiles again when rain
Descends in cool, refreshing streams,
Soothed by that sweet familiar strain
His heated brow with pleasure beams.
He pauses, listens, turns, and bends

Beneath an archway dark and low,
Veiling a path that onward wends
'Mid tangled brake and berries' glow
To where a streamlet murmurs by,
Through the dark forest's colonnade
Arching where nestling violets lie
And light pale torches through the glade.

Here maids and youths are grouped around,
Or in the chequered shadows dance,
Lightly as fairies skim the ground
Beneath the moon's bewitching glance.
And faster speed the dancer's feet,
And castanets more wildly ring,
Louder the silvery timbrels beat,
Closer the arms of Beauty cling,
More liquid grow those flashing eyes,

Deeper the rose on every cheek,
While swifter yet the measure flies,
And hearts their life-long secret speak.

But one there was, whose slender form
Seemed moulded of a finer clay,
A flower unfit to face the storm
That gathers o'er life's fev'rish day.
Pensive that face, whose classic lines
A Grecian statue might have graced,
Stamped with the mind's immortal signs
And all that beauty ever traced.
Her eyes, soft, full, and darkly blue,
Seemed lit at Passion's altar fires:
Beneath their deep and tender hue
There lurked Love's flame that ne'er expires.
And like the spark that leaps to life,

Propelled by Nature's hidden force
To swell the elemental strife
Or speed the lava's fiery course,
In Masaniello's heart arose
A love he strove in vain to hide.
He who had lived to hate his foes,
And e'en the thought of love deride
As some insidious, wily snare
To lure him with a fatal shaft,
Like Syren's smile or goblet fair
That sparkles with a poisoned draught,—
He who had sworn that life should wane
Ere he forgot its only goal,
To free his country from her chain,
The iron that pierced her inmost soul,—
Should *he*, in one brief, sunny hour,
Fling to the winds his cherished scheme

And bow, a slave to beauty's power
As seen in some enchanting dream ?
Keen was the struggle, loud the knell
That conscience echoed in his breast,
He yielded—triumphed—wavered—fell,
For Love his final dart had pressed !
Drawn by that sweet, magnetic force,
Whose sway no earthly limit knows,
Howe'er we strive to shun its course
And quench a flame that ever glows,—
Nearer he stood, breathed Laura's name,
And claimed her for the coming dance,
Powerless now the love to tame
Born of her tender, melting glance.
And while the Tarantella's strains
With all their sweetness fill the air,
While on her throne wild Pleasure reigns

And thrills through every bosom there,
Her ear had caught a whispered word,
Once said a lover ne'er recalls,
Th' impassioned rapturous word she heard
That every woman's heart enthralls.
Pale grew her cheek and quivering met
The lips, that would have sealed his bliss,
But in their tremor faltered yet
To echo language such as this.
And yet her heart was full—of love
She now first felt and could not paint,
Such love, she deem'd, as reigns above,
Pure and unsoiled by earthly taint.

Swift as a meteor darts athwart the skies,
He read the language of those gentle eyes;
The moistened lashes and the flushing cheek,

The tremulous lips their sweet confession speak.
Then in tumultuous, eager, wild embrace
He clasped her form and raised her blushing
face;—
The torturing doubt, the dread suspense was past,
The tempest hushed, the haven found at last!
And now are forged, as moments swiftly roll,
The golden rivets that link soul to soul,
And there reëchoed in those hearts again
Love's sweetest song in one harmonious strain.

A happy presage for a marriage day,
Morn's brightest smiles on fair Sorrento play.
On each pine stem the sun's soft glances rest
And crown with glory every plumèd crest ;
While o'er the vale, in deep and lingering gloom,
The clust'ring grapes unfold their purple bloom.
Thro' many a pathway fringed with myrtle
wreaths,
The tangled briar fragrant incense breathes,
And lemon blossoms with the orange vie
To charm the senses and enchant the eye.

The village bells from yonder lofty tower,
Nestled in ivy of their antique bower,
O'er the fresh breeze a merrier greeting wave
Than ever voice or magic music gave,
As down the curves of a stone-cumbered way

A rustic gathering winds in garments gay,
And sacred banners proudly soar on high
In varied hues of many a brilliant dye ;
On infant brows the festal garlands rest
And new-born roses star each maiden's breast ;
While nuptial hymn and slowly chaunted prayer
Their notes unite and mingle in the air.

And now they halt where glowing colours stain
The time-worn threshold of the sacred fane.
Then o'er the aisles, as if on seraph wings,
Pure voices soar and heavenly music rings,
Now soft and plaintive as a whispered prayer
(The heart's sweet incense wafted on the air),
Now grandly bursting as the torrents sweep
Down the deep furrows of an Alpine steep.
As the last echoes from the altar rise

And melt away in long-drawn, trembling sighs,
The vows are uttered. In that sunny hour
Love opes the portals of his golden bower,
And bids from morn to the decline of day
Each fleeting moment breathe its tender lay.

O'er the smooth tide of Capri's Bay
The moon sheds many a trembling ray,
Like quivering pearls in silver bound,
Or paths in some enchanted ground.
The breath of summer's sweetest flowers
In orange grove and myrtle bowers
Seems fanned from Angel wings above,
Like kisses on the lips of love.
And onward floats the scented gale
To every slow returning sail,
While strains of Tasso's liquid song
On the soft air are borne along.

Yet in this hour of calm and peace
When Nature's throes might seem to cease,
Vesuvius crowned with wreaths of fire
Mutters a warning note of ire ;—

And soon, as if with whirlwinds sown,
Echoes a deep sepulchral moan.
Then, from the crater yawning wide,
O'er the steep mountain's ebon side,
Gathers a spiral stream of flame
Beyond all power of man to tame.
Swelling in volume, breadth and might,
It seems to mock the veil of night,
Illumines valley, hill and plain,
Flashing its image o'er the main,
And wraps the clouds in lurid glow,
As if the Heavens were its foe,
Or on the earth for aye accursed
The very gates of hell had burst.

Still onward sweeps the surging flood,
A mighty river of seething blood,

Breathing its fiery breath around
With a wild, crashing, hissing sound,—
Now rolling towards the leafy trees,
Which bend as if they met the breeze,
Or quailed before the lava's blast,
And shivering felt their die was cast,—
Now sealing on the golden grain
The doom of Sodom's blasted plain,—
Carrying its terrors far and wide
In the full sway of strength and pride,
Till nought but smouldering ashes fill
The place where blushed the vine-clad hill,—
And all is silent, dark and drear,
And only desolation near.

* * * * *

The guards were won,—the drawbridge passed,—
His hand no more the poniard clasped ;—
The gateway gained,—the danger o'er,—
He freely drew his breath once more.
And bright flashed Masaniello's eye
And every throbbing pulse rose high,
For 'neath Anselmo's portal stood
A form in sombre cape and hood,
Whose stalwart limbs full well he knew ;
'Twas one of his own trusty crew,—
And Heav'n itself had deigned to send,
In hour of direst need,—a friend !
" How cam'st thou here, and wherefore ? Say !
" Speak low,—for careless tones betray.
" 'Tis true the Castle guard is won,
" But only till *my* task is done ;
None else can pass,—and none must share

The peril I alone would bear.
"'Tis death to scale this prison wall;
"Can danger ne'er thy heart appal
"That thou should'st risk the wheel, the rack,
"Or even worse? Gonsalvo, back!—
"Lest ere the stars have paled their light,
"Thy head should crown yon turret's height."

"Nay, Masaniello, we are bound
"By stronger ties than kindred found;
"A country's love,—a country's woe,—
"The mightiest links a heart can know.
"Then hear me now. I learnt today
"Thy bark had never skimmed the bay;
"'Twas strange,—for that swift, fleecy sail
"E'er graced the tide in calm or gale.
"All day I scanned the busy streets

"Where thy tall form each passer greets;
"By tower gate,—in market place,
"Vainly I sought thy friendly face.
"What mission could'st thou now fulfil?
"I questioned closely, dreading ill;
"But each new search in vain was made;
"None knew where Masaniello strayed.
"At dusk, by St. Antonio's shrine
"I bent before the Form Divine,
"But scarce had muttered half a prayer,
"When the night-gun broke on the air;
"And, as I saw its flashes light
"The arrow on Anselmo's height,
"Swift as the sound was winged along,
"My thoughts flew to our common wrong;
"An inner voice,—nay what you will,—
"Filled me with fears of coming ill,

"Pointed my course, and seemed to say:
"There's peril to the cause! Away!
"Tonight by yonder castle wall
"A noble patriot chief may fall!—
"Such is my tale,—the rest you know
"Gonsalvo ne'er could shun a foe!"

"Enough!—Full well I've seen thy love for me,
"Thy ardent thirst to set our country free,
"And often prayed the time might not be long
"Ere all, like thee, would hate the bitter wrong,
"The crushing woes, the despot's iron heel,
"With all the frenzy I myself can feel;
"For then alone I hoped to light the flame
"And purge our annals of Oppression's name,
"An altar raise round which our sons should stand
"And bless the hands that had redeemed their land.

"But other purpose brings me here to-day:—
"No plan to ripen and no foes to slay—
"A wife to solace, whose dark-shadowing fears
"Seek deeper vent than in mere idle tears.
"As some fair tendril clasps the parent vine,
"Her gentle heart is close entwined with mine,
"And dreads the dangers that may compass me
"From hidden toils and deeds of treachery,
"With such intentness that her fragile form
"Bends like a reed before the bursting storm,
"And straining chords of a too slender life
"May snap, alas! and end her earthly strife;
"While reft of love,—my beacon,—I may stray,
"A shattered wreck, along my lonely way!
"Thou know'st, Gonsalvo, that the despot's chain
"Has laid on Laura its full weight of pain.
"Without the semblance of a trial, doomed

"Within these walls to be for months entombed,
"Where slimy worms and vermin's noxious brood
"Crawl out and fatten, e'en on prison food,—
"Where scarce a glimmer of the light of day
"Sheds through the bars a pale and sickly ray,
"And scarce a breath of heavy, fetid air
"Stirs the frail fabric of the spider's lair!
"Suffice to tell thee that the human mind
"Could scarce imagine torture more refined.
"And canst thou doubt such wrongs will swell the tide
"That shall o'erwhelm our tyrants far and wide,
"And, every sorrow, every struggle o'er,
"Plant Freedom's standard on our native shore?
"But now to Laura, e'er the darkness grows,
"Lest time should fail us to escape our foes."

With muffled step and cautious gaze he led
Down a steep stair where ne'er the sun had
shed
His cheering rays; but lit by pallid lamp
Each dark step showed green, slippery hues of
damp,
And massive walls whereon the mildew lay
In dull grey streaks, as if to mark the way.
And now they reached a gate fixed in the stone,
The last great bar athwart the dungeon
thrown,
Scarred with the blows of many an iron mace,
Like hardened wrinkles on a prison face.
The giant hinges turned without a sound
(Unbarred by friendly jailor on his round)
And a dim, lurid glimmer scarce revealed
The cell where Laura's cruel fate was sealed.

Her's was a face that few could e'er forget.
More classic lines you might in truth have met,
But none where Love and Poesy could sign
In clearer letters all their gifts divine.
Wrapt in a trance—the soul's mysterious sleep,
Where wakeful dreams a sacred vigil keep—
Her gaze seemed fixed on regions far away,
Lit by the light of some unearthly day.
The marble features, bloodless, thin, and drawn,
Cold as the snow in northern climes at dawn,
Mirror'd the image of that crushing grief
For which no words could ever bring relief.
The fingers locked, transparent as the light,
And pale as moonbeams on a summer's
night,
Held Masaniello's latest words of love
And seemed to lift them to the Throne above,

While the loosed tresses of her raven hair
Fell like a pall o'er that unuttered prayer.

One glance he gave and softly clasped
The hands his loving missive grasped,—
And fast and warm the kisses fell
As if to print a long farewell.
Then round her form his arms were thrown,
With all the ardour love alone
Like his could feel; such passion's glow
None but true hearts can ever know;
A balm the deepest wound to heal
O'er which despair has set her seal,—
The burst of sunshine thro' the cloud,—
The garland that illumes the shroud,—
For such he deem'd that mute embrace
As he surveyed her pallid face.

The saddened eyes still rayless seemed
And wrapt in sleep, as if she dreamed.
An anguished cry,—a bitter groan,—
The manly heart's long prisoned moan—
Escaped him ; and full well they told
The agony as yet controlled.
"Laura ! dear Laura ! sweetest bride,
"Look on me, love,"—he wildly cried,—
"Come to these arms ;—they yearn to press
"Thy form with passion's warm caress ;
"And let me pour into thine ear
"The oft-told tale thou lov'st to hear !"

Slow as the thin grey mists of dawn
Roll from the earth to greet the morn,
Fleeted the shades of Laura's night,—
And radiant gleams broke o'er her brain

Melting the spirit's icy chain,
To lead it back to realms of light.
And as he marked the cheek's soft hue,
The lips once more o'erspread with dew,
The diamonds that had paled their rays
With brilliant light illume her gaze,—
That life suspended draw its breath
And tear away the veil of death,
He felt that Heaven his fate had blest,
And signed the Cross upon his breast.
"My own,—my husband,—dearest life!
"Is it in truth thyself I see?
"And art thou come to set me free—
"Thy loving, true, devoted wife—
"From this abhorred and galling chain
"That seems to pierce my soul and brain,
"Till even Memory's sweetest leaves

"Are withered like the sun-dried sheaves,
"And all my loyal love for thee
"Sinks in a gulf of misery?"

"Oh! loved one, strive for strength to bear
"The load I fain would with thee share.
"Take heart! for soon the hour will come
"(The sign, a muffled roll of drum)
"When thro' the city's silent streets,
"Where'er a patriot bosom beats,
"Freedom's fair torch shall brightly shine,
"And hireling curs may howl and whine.
"Then, gathering round the Chief they chose
"For the fierce hate he bears their foes,
"Our men shall bare their blades for fight;
"'Mid ringing cheers that rend the sky
"A thousand hands shall wave on high,

"A thousand poniards leap to light!
"And then, my love, thy chains must fall
"Felled by the blow that ends our thrall,
"And thou, pale image of our wrongs,
"Shalt grace our proud triumphant throngs,
"Whose swelling shouts on high proclaim
"The People's rights,—the Tyrant's shame!"

And, as he spoke, a roseate glow,
Like evening's blush on Alpine snow,
Stole o'er her breast, that rose and fell
Beneath love's pure and magic spell,
As if the beating heart within
Would burst its bonds and freedom win.

Then, as he raised her in a close embrace
And fondly pressed that agitated face,

The moon illumined with her mystic beams
Those cold grey walls that seemed to mock their
dreams,
While the pale light of the soft evening star
Shed holy greetings from bright worlds afar.

"The star of Hope is shining in the skies
"To dry thy tears,—to hush thy bitter sighs.
"Look up, my love, and meet those cheering
rays!
"They bode thy freedom, speak of happier days;
"No bars impede yon messages of love;
"They come unfettered from the courts above
"To smile alike upon the Monarch's halls
"And the cold cells within these prison walls.
"And now, farewell!—Oh! wing a prayer on high
"For him who loves thee and perchance may die

"Breathing thy name with his last fainting breath,—
"True to thee, living,—true to thee in death!"
Once more he drew her closely to his breast,
Once more her lips with love's sweet signet pressed,
Then waved adieu. . . . . . .

Gonsalvo by his side?
Where was he now? and where his love,—his bride?
Had one brief hour of tumultuous joy
(Though mixed with moments of griefs dark alloy)
Sufficed to menace even Reason's throne?
Yes, save Gonsalvo, he was now alone.—
Thus much he felt, but aching heart and brain

Were well nigh crushed beneath their load of
pain.
He hardly marked the outlets of the tower,
The hated ensigns of the despot's power,
The guard and drawbridge he had scanned but
now
With flashing eye and with close knitted brow;
His onward course he never seemed to heed,
And only spoke to bid Gonsalvo speed.

Onward they dash in headlong, mad career,—
One aim—one thought—the city gates to near;
While thousand torches stamp their lurid seal
On sunburnt face or fiercely brandished steel,
Shrill shouts on high for speedy vengeance soar,
And savage curses swell the deaf'ning roar.
The barriers shattered that their course would
    stay,
The guards disarmed whom they disdain to slay,
The ducal shield beneath their heelprints crush'd,
The standard torn, dishonour'd, stain'd with dust,
The cannon spiked, the matchlocks seized and
    shared,
The guard-house fired that resistance dared;
Still from those ranks rose the impassioned cry:
"On—till our tyrants yield to us or die!"—
Past long arcade, by shadow-peopled square

And sleep-hushed palace woke by din and glare,
Thro' winding passage where the torch reveals
That thick set darkness the night wanderer feels,
By low-browed arch and dome-roofed colonnade,
Where the sun's beams can never pierce the
shade,
The loud sharp echo of those hurrying feet
Arouse to life each still, deserted street.
At length they reach the castle's moated wall,
Whose strength may baffle but can ne'er appal
Those hearts that vibrate with one measured beat,
Taught but to conquer, and to scorn retreat.
The ladders planted and the onset timed,
As the last carbine rings the signal "primed,"
With a wild rush the counterscarp they scale,
And many a volley wings its leaden hail.
Hurled back they waver—rally—onward press—

Once more fall back—their ranks still closer
dress ;
While gunshot wounds, that ghastly shapes define,
The band diminish to a single line.
Again their ranks with lightning speed they form
Despite the fury of the bullets' storm ;—
Then with a shout in serried mass they charge,
As the spent powder hurls its last discharge,
Break thro' their foes, and give no quarter,—slay,
Till all are vanquished,—and they win the day.
From the dark summit of the belfry tower
The bells proclaim their first triumphant hour,—
But in those muffled, deep and mournful tones
That seem to echo a whole nation's groans.

* * * * *

From yonder high cathedral tower
The chimes proclaim the midnight hour.
Save for the notes of music low
That silvery from the organ flow,
Now in softest cadence sigh,
Now in wilder accents die,
A solemn stillness reigns around
Such as befits that hallowed ground;
For shriven souls are gathered there,
And every heart is wrapt in prayer.
Now thro' the dim, deep-shadowed aisle,
Where contrite breasts confess their guile,
Glides Masaniello. His thoughts are rife
With deeds of blood and scenes of strife;
And in that restless, eager gaze
Illumined still with piercing rays,
That never quailed, that knew no fear,

Now lurks a sense of danger near,—
The final stake for life or death.
So quickly came his fleeting breath,
So throbbed his heart, so swelled each
vein,
Their very tension gave him pain.
The wasted limbs, the halting pace,
The bloodshot eye and haggard face,
Where lawless acts of deepest dye
Are graved in lines that cannot lie,—
Sorrows that wring the inmost soul
As hours on hours onward roll,
Till Reason e'en withholds her light,
And the mind sinks in darkest night,—
Such tokens the dread truth betray
That few dared e'en in whisper say.

He turned and bent before a shrine,
Then paused—was it the holy Sign,—
Or Faith, that darkest perils breed,
Bade him the voice of conscience heed?
If so, 'twas but a transient gleam
Too soon, alas! to shroud its beam.
His hands are now too deep in blood,
Each day must swell th' ensanguined flood.
With lips compressed and haughty mien
He felt his poniard's edges keen,
The ample sash still tighter rolled
That knit his mantle's ample fold,—
Then passed into a secret cell
(Witness of many a martyr's knell),
Where safe, he deemed, from all his foes,
Wearied and worn, he sought repose.
But for the deep and measured breath,

Rigid his form as if in death.
Anon he started—shuddered—groaned,
As if his soul its sins bemoaned.
Was it a dream? Or did his ear
In truth an awful summons hear?—
He rose,—looked out upon the bay
Where fisher barks at anchor lay,
And clear, as if ne'er veiled in night,
Back o'er his brain flashed Reason's light.—
Again his features wore the seal
Of all that mind and soul reveal.
He swiftly glanced o'er mem'ry's page
From childhood—youth—to riper age;
How he had loved to set his sail
And bid defiance to the gale,
Fling wide his net, the waves survey,—
His home,—the deep, blue-breasted bay,—

Scene of all pleasure, peril, strife,
Birthplace of love and e'en of life,
Where first his schemes of Freedom sprung,
And Friendship's kindly hand was wrung.
Dear to his soul each rock and isle
Lit with the warm and sunny smile
That seemed to tell of song and mirth
And make a Paradise of Earth.
How his heart yearned for that still shore,
To bound across the wave once more,
Feel that at least his soul was free
And heir of immortality,—
Howe'er on earth he might despair,
Howe'er condemned to shipwreck there!

Why wear his thoughts this gloomy hue?
Why breathe his trembling lips "Adieu'

Why pale his cheek and damp his brow?
Why quivers every fibre now?
Was it that inner whisp'ring voice
That dimly bids our hearts rejoice
Or mourn, now wildly cling to hope,
Now with despair and darkness cope,
As if some dread and mystic sign
Were given by the Hand Divine?

But now quick steps the night's deep silence break
And clash of arms their ringing echoes wake,
While oaths and murmurs, shouts and frantic cries
In loud, confused, tumultuous discord rise.
Nearer they come, as if some wild affray
To his lone cell would force its savage way,
And 'mid the roar of that o'erwhelming flood
Sate fiercest passions in a sea of blood.

Hate at his heart and fury in his eyes,
As on his foe the hunted tiger flies,
One bound he gave, and burst the iron door
To meet his fate,—defy or hush the roar.
Such were the thoughts that flashed across his
brain.
A moment more,—they were dispelled again ;
Above that din he seemed to hear his name :
Friends were at hand ; to greet their Chief they
came!
Fast beat his heart with mad excitement now,
And exultation shone upon his brow,
For these were shouts for new-born ventures won,
Or plans of triumph for tomorrow's sun.

Scarce had those sounds in joyous accents rung,
To dome and aisle in long vibrations clung,—

When from the depths of a dim, shadowy arch
A dark and threatening form with stealthy march
Moved phantom like. But ah! ne'er phantom showed
Such deadly purpose, with like passion glowed.
In hooded cloak of sable hue arrayed,
Whose treacherous folds the glittering arms betrayed,
Onward *it* moved,—at Masaniello gazed,—-
Stood still,—drew back,—and then a weapon raised.
Gleamed the bright flash and flew the deadly ball
With hissing sound;—an anguished groan—a fall,—
And Treachery's hand with one faint stream of blood

'Whelmed Victory's tide e'er it had reached the
flood,—
Shattered all hope,—for ever broke the spell,—
As, basely murdered, Masaniello fell.
Now feebly struggling in the grasp of death,
"Traitor" he murmured with fast fleeting breath;
A quivering gasp—a muttered word—a sigh!
Then all was still; a film obscured the eye,
And o'er that pallid, prostrate, stiffening form
Had swept Earth's final, ruin-freighted storm;
On gentle wings the Spirit soared above,
To sue for mercy at the Throne of Love.

Still o'er the livid, lifeless clay
Lingered the soul's last parting ray,
And seemed to paint its long adieu
In colours of ethereal hue,

And lend a pure and matchless grace
To that now pale and placid face,
As if, e'er yet the form were cold,
To cast each line in Heaven's mould.

Ask not of Death where soars the soul
Unrobed of flesh, where lies its goal,
The final mystic place of rest?
Ask not its judgment—cursed or blest:
'Twere vain to seek man's final doom
Beyond the cruel, silent tomb.
No mortal hand can break the seal;
No mind that hidden fate reveal;
The quickened form must rise again
To learn the secret of its pain,
The dark-dyed source of sin to know
And all its heritage of woe.

Then may those tears be wiped away
That dimmed the Patriot's brightest day ;
His be to hear a joyful sound
Proclaimed on God's most holy ground,
The sentence by the crystal sea,—
A crown of Immortality !

POEMS.

E

POETRY AND LOVE.

THE roseate hues that wreathe the setting sun,
Ere twilight comes to tell his course is run,
And night steeps nature in the sleep of death
Till dawn awakes it with her gentle breath ;
The silvery streaks that tinge the shadowy vales,
When o'er the sky the moon in triumph sails,
And yields her light in one unclouded stream
Till earth and heaven in one glory gleam ;
The dimpled cheek of ocean laid to rest,
When trembling stars are mirrored on its breast
The smile of morning in the early spring
When all the woods with joyous carols ring ;
The kiss of summer wafted on the gale

From fragrant shrubs that mantle hill and vale,
When the first dew-drops shed their gentle shower
And sprinkle diamonds on each opening flower;
The measured cadence of the boatman's oar
That whispers music to the silent shore,
And softly wakes those streams of living light
To gild the waters as they fade from sight;
The notes that vibrate thro' some Gothic pile,
When swelling anthems fill the fretted aisle,
Where brightest tints of many a varied shade
Stain the rich marbles where the great are laid—
Such are the scenes that earth and art unroll,
And such the sounds that chain the poet's soul.

But who shall say, 'tis *then* his breast is stirred
By sweetest strains that mortal ear hath heard?
Or e'en that scenes that most enthrall the eye

Can with the love of tender woman vie?

Those golden links, that join to bind the heart,

No weight can weaken and no force can part;

Tho' earthly trials mighty efforts make,

The chain may bend,—but not a link can break.

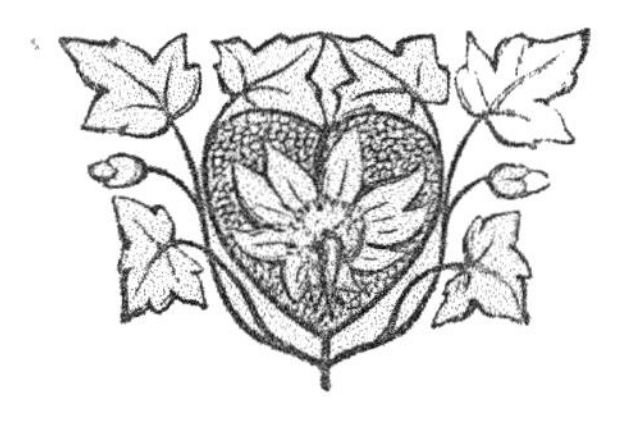

THE OLD JOURNAL.

Poor faded leaves! nay, let them lie;
My cheeks would only glow
To read of happy days gone by,
And bitter tears would flow.

Records of hours whose hallowed gleams
Shed brightness o'er my soul!
Dearer each word, each sentence seems
As years still onward roll.

That withered rose still marks the page
We read by gleaming tide,—
A legend of the golden age,
Life's bright and sunny side.

The perfume lingers on the leaves,
Though sere and faded now,
Sweet as the visions Fancy weaves
To cheer the clouded brow.

Days may be dreary, dark and chill,
Hearts dear to me grow cold,—
These leaves will throw around me still
The scent they gave of old.

And o'er yon blotted lines will shine
The halo of the past,
When *his* loved hand was clasped in mine
And I was his at last.

Nay, let me read them once again ;—
We *cannot* say farewell.

Those words soothe aching heart and brain,
Though sad the tale they tell.

Oft as I weep thus here alone
I dream he lives once more,
And then he whispers, " Hush thy moan :
" We meet on Heaven's shore ! "

Soft to my ear bright seraphs wing
His melodies of love,
And then I think I hear him sing
From the golden gates above !

A DREAM OF A LOST SOUL.

I stood alone amid the shades of night,
And all around a death-like silence reigned.
Anon pale flashes of a lurid light
With crimson hues the shadowy valleys stained;
And o'er the crags, whose jagged summits glowed
Like fiery spectres from some mystic world,
In violet robes the mists of Heaven rode,
By silent winds with lightning swiftness hurled.
Beyond the plain, in deeper darkness veiled,
I saw the billows of a restless sea,
That 'neath the beams of silvery planets paled
And seemed to bound the vast immensity.
Yet nearer lay broad wastes of gleaming sand,

'Mid grey rocks rent by some convulsion's wave,
While storm-swept forests rose on either hand,
Chill, dark and dreary as the cruel grave.
The dim-lit moon I deemed enthroned on high
To mourn for man ;—for every living breath
Had yielded up a last and lingering sigh
And left its echoes in this vale of death.
Where'er I gazed, on pathless wild and wold,
Where never sun had lent its golden light,
I saw dim shades fast flitting, wan and cold,
That shed around them an o'erwhelming blight.
A kindred spirit stirred my stony heart
To swell the train of that unhallowed band,
And seemed to whisper, I must bear my part
In that wild, wasted and forsaken land.
And then I felt how bitter was my doom,—
For this, the sentence of eternal woe :

To spread around impenetrable gloom
And evil seeds of desolation sow.
I joined the shades that quickly gathered round
To breathe destruction's unrelenting blast,
And rose on wings that cleaved without a sound
Those airless regions, and no shadows cast.
Time had no limits, and our realms no bourne,—
And ever on through endless cycles swept
Our wild array, by every passion torn
That ne'er relented nor a moment slept.
What anguish thrilled our ever restless throng,
As through the plains of endless space above
We heard the music of the seraph's song,
Now raised in triumph and now hushed in love!—
Then through the long illumined aisles of thought
We saw the drama of our lives unroll,
And all the wrong our evil hearts had wrought

With fresh remorse o'erwhelmed the stricken soul.
To silence doomed and never-ceasing toil,
To vain regret and unavailing prayer,
Around the heart our chain of sin to coil,
And sink beneath the weight of wild despair!
Those living waters now for ever dried,
The gates of Mercy by the Angels barred,
The spirit forced from Heaven's light to hide,
The essence sullied, and the Image marred!

WAR AND PEACE.

From sea to sea, from shore to shore,
Hark to the cannon's mighty roar!
Wild horsemen dash,
Bright sabres clash,
And legions down on legions pour.

Hark! to the crashing shot and shell
That plough the plain and pierce the dell;
That stifled groan,—
That anguished moan
Too well their own sad story tell.

See yonder banner steeped in gore,—
The blackened roof,—the crimsoned floor,—

Dark heaps of slain,—
The harvest's stain!
Hark to the cannon's mighty roar!

* * * * *

But now, o'er plain, o'er hill and vale,
The blood-red hues of slaughter pale;
An Angel sings,
Peace spreads her wings,
And Hope unbends her sunny sail.

Where'er the eye can scan the space,
The golden fields earth's bosom grace;
With lowing kine
The meadows shine,
And smiles illumine Nature's face.

'Tis Peace—'tis peace! from shore to shore
No longer sounds the cannon's roar.
O'er mound and grave
The olive wave!
The sword be sheathed for evermore!

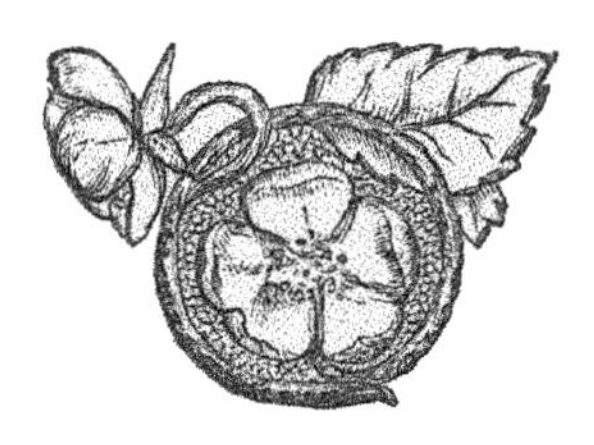

THE WRECK.

I stood on yonder rocky crest,
  Where storm-beat sea-gulls rise ;
Across the ocean's surging breast
  I strained my weary eyes.

With yearning heart I watched the sail
  Cleave thro' the billows' foam,
And prayed that God would stay the gale
  And bear him safely home.

The bending masts and dipping prow
  A farewell seemed to wave. . . . . .
(Scarce can I breathe it even now)—
  They pointed to the grave!

In one brief moment, all of life
  And joy and hope had fled ;—
I felt that o'er that Tempest's strife
  My life's last rays were shed.

TO M. L.

In those long weary hours, love,
When I am far from thee,
My life is but a desert, love,
With no green spot for me.

How ardently I long, my love,
For that sweet face of thine,
To fold thee in these arms, my love,
And feel that thou art mine!

To meet thy tender kisses, love,
And stay them in their flight,
To play with thy dark tresses, love,
That shine with liquid light!

To tell thee thou art dearer, love,
Than any one on earth,
To share thy little sorrows, love,
Or join thee in thy mirth !

In those long weary hours, love,
When I am far from thee,
I feel like some lone raft, my love,
Or bark on angry sea,

Torn by the winter blast, my love,
And swept by every wave,
Till sinking in the depths, my love,
It finds a silent grave.

But happier, happier far, my love,
When those sad hours go by,

I find my quiet haven, love,
My bright and sunny sky.

For where thy smiles are seen, my love,
All clouds are chased away,
And every moment seems, my love,
Like one long Summer day.

TO THE ZITHER.

I heard a voice with touching pathos breathe
Sweet, thrilling notes as Angels sing above;
Around my soul those accents seemed to wreathe
The tender bonds of an immortal love.
And ere their echoes on the ear had died
Those last vibrations filled my heart with pain.
It was as if a sorrowing voice replied:
"Farewell for aye: we never meet again."—
And then deep sadness o'er my spirit fell;
Unbidden tears upon mine eyelids rose,
For those sad chords of sorrows seemed to tell
That round the path of every being close.

And then I heard a stirring prelude ring,
And break in gladness like a summer morn.
'Twas *then* I felt the heart can sometimes sing
And from life's sorrows for a while be torn,—
Now melt in softness, as a lover's prayer,
And mirror peace like some lake's placid breast,—
Now, reft of joy, the veil of sorrow wear
Till the last throb proclaims its endless rest.

THE GUARDIAN ANGELS.

Yes! the mystic cords are wove:
Bonds of Heaven link the Earth;
Round us ever Angels rove
Smiling on us from our birth.

In the breezeless calm of Night,
In that reign of peace below,
When the stars are flashing light
And the moonbeams softly glow,—

When all sighs are hushed in sleep,
And the voice of woe is still,—
Then the Angels vigil keep
And the air with whispers fill

(Whispers that of solace tell,
Words that breathe of love and rest),—
Working each a silent spell,
Healing every wounded breast,

Guiding with a Heavenly ray,
Sheltering 'neath their unseen wings,
Pointing upward to the way
Where the seraph-choir sings.

THE CHRISTIAN MARTYR.

(ON THE PICTURE OF PAUL DELAROCHE).

The sighing wind is hushed in sleep,
And stillness settles on the deep;
Midnight has steeped in darker hue
The vault of heaven's deepest blue;
The very stars have veiled their sheen
And seem to mourn their absent queen.
The mountains wrapped in misty shrouds
Frown on the shore like tempest clouds,
Or forms of the forgotten dead,
Dread spectres of the spirit fled.

Around,—on high,—an ever growing gloom,—
The solemn silence of the peaceful tomb,—

Save where the mew her fleeting shadow
flings
And makes faint music with her snowy
wings.

So still the scene,—so hush'd the air,
We almost doubt that life is there!
Nature proclaims her reign of rest
And breathes a calm o'er ev'ry breast,
Bids passion quench her flaming brand
And crime withhold her bloody hand,—
The penitential prayer to rise
And waft its incense to the skies.
For cold the heart and tame the soul
That views these boundless waters roll,
The earth below, the heavens above,
And feels no spark of holy love!

Lo! thro' the gathering darkness gleams
A wreath of light (the brightest beams
That ever radiant moon hath lent
To gild the wondrous firmament l).
Nearer it glides,—and ocean's cheek
Is tinged with many a tender streak,
Until each softly swelling line
Forms an illumined silver mine.
Now in its course it seems to rest . . .
Great God! it lights a woman's breast!—
Hush! breathe not with the faintest breath!
Those saintly eyes are closed in death,
No more to smile, to win, to weep,
No more their weary watch to keep,—
Sealed in their long and last repose,
For ever sealed, to friends and foes,

Till opening at the Seraph's strain
They meet Christ's holy ransomed train.

The crimson flow, the lacerating thong,
Bear silent witness of the foulest wrong.
Upon that breast of dazzling marble hue
The arms are crossed,—in silence seem to sue
For all that prayer e'er asked, or mercy gave,
For rest,—for pardon,—peace beyond the grave.
Yon halo tells how Martyrdom hath won
The crown,—the glory of the Blessed Son!

FAREWELL.

Oh! whisper it gently . . . . As it dies on the ear,
The well-springs of sorrow in bitterness flow,
For the heart feels the winter of life must be near,
And the hour of parting no solace can know.

Gone—gone are those moments too fleeting and brief,
Like the skies' mantling blush at the set of the sun,
When we met in your home to share pleasure and
grief,
Ere Time's golden sands their swift courses had run.

Oh! whisper it gently . . . . As the sad echo falls
On the keen listening ear, like a withering blight,
A tear dims the eye, for the dread knell recalls
The days that have fled as a watch in the night.

Yet the frail silver chord, when it parts from the lyre,
Gives a lingering sigh as it struggles with death,
And that tender adieu loses none of its fire
That is wafted away in its last dying breath.

Ever onward it speeds, as its melody rings
And mingles with strains that have soared in the sky,
Since music first rose on her heavenly wings
To charm all the earth and the angels on high.

So memory graves on the shrine of the heart
The days gone for ever,—too happy to last ;—
What though Fortune decree that henceforth we must
part,
In our minds are embalmed the sweet thoughts of the
Past !

THE TOURNAMENT.

The earth shines forth in glory 'neath a sky of deepest blue,
And sparkle leaf and flower bright all diamonded with dew;
A range of lofty pine-clad hills in plumy vesture gleams,
And on their deeply shadowed crests the eye of Heaven beams.
Here, throned in every manly breast, the Queen of Beauty smiles,
And with her voice's melody the vacant hour beguiles;
Here many a dame of proud descent and maid of high degree

Are gathered round above the lists, the goodly show
to see;
Here glance the eyes of Southern France and Britain's
milk-white brows;
Here damask cheeks with blushes glow that love's
soft whispers rouse;
Here flash the witty repartee and laughter's joyous
ring,
And every heart on pleasure bent with joyance seems
to sing.

Now all is changed,—and Beauty's lips in silence
deep are bound;
The lists are thronged with champions brave,—the
heralds stand around;
They crave a moment's silence, and in loud accents
name

Each belted Knight in order, his lineage and his
fame.
And as the eager combatants in turn their coursers
wheel
To fill their destined stations, 'mid the din of clashing
steel,
The streamers of the lances o'er their helmets' plum-
age wave,
And the sun's bright rays each corselet with golden
facets pave.

Thrice through the crowded lists is heard the herald's
warning cry:
"Do your devoirs, ye noble Knights, to conquer or
to die;
"Man dies but once, oh! mark ye well, but Glory
lives for aye;

"Bright eyes are gazing on you now, your mighty
deeds survey.
"Let none disturb this combat fair by force or
slander's breath,
"Or he shall surely meet his doom, the well earned
meed of death."

And now the gage of battle fierce is hurled upon the
ground,
The stalwart barriers open wide, and shouts,—'On
On!' resound;—
While far across the peaceful vale the trumpet's note
is heard,
Each cheek with ardour crimsons, and each breast is
deeply stirred;
Each lance's point is levelled low and placed within
its rest;

The bridle firmly grasped anew, the steed with spur
is pressed;
And, each helmet set well downward, they charge in
full career,
Those trusty Knights of wide renown, without
reproach or fear.
And the shock of every ónset was like dark clouds
that fly
To mar the fairest spots of earth with weapons forged
on high.

The dust by trampling coursers raised has mantled
all the air,
And into gloom and darkness changed the light
of morning fair,
While eager eyes are strained around, and every
heart beats fast,

To read upon the ensanguined field the die that had been cast.

No nobler line of Chivalry had ever poised a lance,

And sad the scene now full revealed to every anxious glance :—

The steed without its rider,—the helm without its plume,—

The shattered lance and broken crest,—the plain of death and gloom.

Some lay in dented armour there, unhorsed, with bleeding breast ;

Some, stiffened by the hand of death, had found a warrior's rest ;

Some vainly strove to staunch their wounds with scarfs fair hands had tied,

And muttered touching farewell words to distant spouse or bride ;

While others, veiled in dust and gore, still strove
with axe or sword
To rival deeds of bravery in knightly annals
stored.

And when the moon's pale shadows fell on yonder
dreary field,
And every fallen warrior had been called to die or
yield,
There went up through the still night air a woman's
bitter wail,
A sound at which e'en hero hearts are sometimes fain
to quail.—
The lady fair of Beauty now, her locks with dewdrops
sown,
With gesture wild and vacant stare, was wandering
there alone ;

Hard by her heart lay buried,—yes! hard by her love
was ta'en,—
Weep for her reason wrecked to-day;—weep for the
hero slain!

THE MINISTRY OF ANGELS.

At the first faint flash of dawn,—
By the eve's last quivering ray,—
When the veil of Heaven is drawn
And the night fades into day,—
Gentle spirits leave the sky,
O'er our homes in silence rise,
Shining like the stars on high,
Watching with sweet, pensive eyes.
Now they spread their healing wings
By the widow's shattered hearth,
And the fount of solace springs
Round her life's deserted path.
Now they stray where orphans sigh
That the thread of life should part,
And the floods of anguish dry

In the mourner's sorrowing heart.
Now they hover round the bed
Where some young hearts softly sleep,
And their prayers are mutely said
While a tender watch they keep.
Theirs to shelter,—theirs to guide
Where our steps may lead astray,—
And be ever by our side,
Stars by night and suns by day.
By the joyful marriage bell,
Ever watching, ever near,—
By the solemn funeral knell,—
In each hour's smile or tear,—
Theirs to lead the thoughts above
To those realms of endless day,
Where, in God's unfading Love,
All our tears are wiped away!

TO M. B.

When the morning of gladness has dawned upon thee,
And thy days from all cares and all sorrows are free;
When the bright joys of home are encircling thy hours
And wreathing thy paths with the fairest of flowers;
When the smile of a sister is beaming on thee
With a love that is deep as the depths of the sea;
When thy soul is enthralled by the magic of mind,
Or by strains of sweet music that float on the wind;
When the first kiss of Spring gives fresh life to the
trees,—
When the last sigh of Summer has perfumed the
breeze,—
When the spoils of the Autumn encumber the
ground,—

When the earth in the ice-chains of Winter is bound;—
In the hush of the night,—in the blush of the morn,—
When thy thoughts on the wings of the lightning are
borne,—
When thy foot treads the chamber or presses the
sod;—
When thy true heart is breathing a prayer to thy
God;—
Oh! then mingle my name with the thoughts of the
hour!
Oh! deck the dark grave of the past with a flower!

THE WATERS' MEET.*

Soft blows the breeze ; the silvery clouds
Are floating o'er their sapphire fields ;
A purple veil the mountain shrouds
And with its fringe the valley shields.

Now lends the sun his morning beams
To light the forest's deepest hold ;
On every leaf and stem there gleams
A radiant flood of purest gold.

A wood-girt river threads the vale,
Folds to its breast the jewelled beams,
Flooding with foam the trout that sail
And sport amid its smiling streams.

* Near Lynton, North Devon.

Far as the eye can reach below,
The flashing waters burst their way ;
O'er tangled brake and fern they flow
And force the rocks to own their sway.

'Mid mountain ash and stately elm
Ten thousand oaks their branches wave,
Leal guardians of the river's realm ;
Their lofty crests the tempests brave.

On, pilgrim ! through enchanted ways,
Meet for the Kelpie's midnight rites,
'Neath gnarlèd stems, by mossy braes,
O'er grassy knolls and heathered heights.

Then pause upon the velvet isle
That smiles above yon gleaming falls,

And seems to bid you rest awhile
Ere yet you view those magic halls.

Embowered in their wooded home,
Lo! rushing waters onward sweep,
And surge, and swell with fleecy foam,
Like billows of the angry deep.

In vain the rocks broad barriers lay,
In vain they group in serried ranks,—
Their jagged sides but sear the spray
That breaks upon the mossy banks.

No life to share the pearls of price
That grace the valley's secret bowers;
Its rocky paths and streams entice
No witness save the silent flowers.

But for the breath that sweeps the gorse,
Or drop that bows the tender blade,
No stir save in the shadow's course
That fitful wanders thro' the glade.

Mark where the river's broadest zone
Channels the wood, to turn aside
And swiftly seize the valley's throne,
As trysting-place to meet his bride!

Here in one close and fond embrace
The streams entwine their arms of snow;
Side pressed to side, and face to face,
They swear for evermore to flow.

IN SORROW'S HOUR.

He's gone!—no more that loving hand
Will press my fevered brow;
He's gone to God's mysterious land,
And life is worthless now.

No more his gentle smile can play
O'er this sweet home of Love;
No more those eyes can meet the day
The deep blue skies above.

Mute is that voice whose tender tone
Once filled my heart with joy;
The pulse is still,—the soul has flown
Where bliss hath no alloy.

He's gone! O God! how dark my days,
That once were bright and clear,
Without those cheering, kindly rays
That shone when *he* was near!

Oh! bind his brows with lilies bright
From Thy wide fields on high,
And robe him with çelestial light
In Thy unclouded sky!

Oh! waft me where his Spirit dwells,
And earthly sorrows cease;
Lead me where Thine Evangel tells
Of endless rest and peace!

THE ZITHER.

Soul-stirring chords! your tender, magic spell
Enthralls the heart and captive binds the ear;
In cadence soft those echoes softly swell,
Like music wafted from the Heavenly sphere.

Now gently trembling as the plaintive notes
That linnets breathe upon the perfumed bough,
Now gently rising as a banner floats
Borne on the breeze above bright Pleasure's prow.

When on the ocean in eve's calmest hour
That liquid music vibrates thro' my breast,
I seem transported to some Angel's bower,
Where sorrows cease, and all is calm and rest.

TO THE PRINCESS A—— M——.

Sweet eyes! that shed a radiant light around
And seem to hallow ev'ry spot of ground,—
Reflecting heaven's softest summer hue;
A soul is mirror'd in that azure blue!

They tell the tale of innocence and youth,
They speak the language of undying truth;—
So pure, so gentle, and so crystal-clear,—
Such eyes were fitted for a better sphere.

Like music wafted o'er the silent sea,
Like chimes that echo thro' the smiling lea,
Or sunbeam glancing on a mountain-stream,—
They lead the thoughts into some mystic dream,
Where all is changed, as by the enchanter's rod,
And angels wear th' immortal crowns of God.

THE LETTER L.

(AN IMITATION).

It heralds our life and the birth of our love,
And lingers for ever with angels above;
It owns not the darkness but ushers the light,
And rests in the cloud, yet is ever in flight.
'Tis the portal of learning, the pivot of health,
The torch of our gloom and the stay of our wealth.
Deserting the lover, it utters his knell,
Yet stoops in true mercy to echo farewell.
While the note of its music in melody rings,
It folds round the lonely its love-laden wings.
Tho' veiled in the hour when the day star appears,
'Tis seen when it wanes in the heavenly spheres;

Without it no balm and no solace are found,
And life is a void and the world but a sound.
It scorns the wide ocean to rule o'er the land;
Each leaf owns its sway and each flower its hand;
Bright rivulets murmur its name as they flow,
And the hills with its impress unceasingly glow.
'Tis enthroned far on high in the halls of the blest,
Yet abides where the wicked shall never find rest.

IN MEMORIAM.

Rest! Rest in peace! All hallowed be thy tomb!
Immortal glory gilds its silent gloom.
Spotless the raiment that enfolds thy form,
Borne far away above life's raging storm!
Radiant the crown that binds thy temples now!
Celestial light beams on the Conqueror's brow.

Rest, victor, rest!—Thy earthly strife is done,
Thy path illumined by a fadeless sun;
Heaven's golden portals open wide for thee
By the great Throne above the crystal sea,
Where tears are dried, where cares and sorrows cease,
'Mid endless raptures and unbroken peace.

Rest, victor, rest!—And may our prayers avail
To calm the anguish of the mourner's wail,
And guide us all through lives as pure as thine
To those bright realms where ransomed spirits shine,
And Angel hosts, whose shouts of triumph ring
For Christ the Saviour and for Christ the King!

THE SUMMONS TO HEAVEN.

Ho! Christian, arise from the dust of the grave!
Thy Saviour is near thee to greet and to save.
The trump of Jehovah is sounding on High
To lead thee to glory. Thy Saviour is nigh.

Lo! legions of Angels are gathered around
To welcome the weary, to joy o'er the found;
The last of the vials of wrath is outpoured;
The lyres are strung for the Feast of the Lord.

The body for aye shall be freed from its dust;
Thy brows shall be bound with the wreath of the just;
The songs of the blest shalt thou sing to thy God;
Thy footsteps shall tread where the holy have trod.

The glories of Heaven revealed shalt thou see;
Each mansion shall open its portals to thee,
Where Angels whose faces no mortals have seen
Shall shine with a halo of heavenly sheen.

With thy wings shalt thou sever the infinite space,
The paths of thy angel-companions to trace,
And with them to feast on Love's Mystical Food,
On pleasures that God has prepared for the good.

Each loved one on earth whom His mercy hath saved,
Whose sins in the Blood of the Saviour are laved,
With the impress of Heaven for aye shall be sealed
And share in the glories no lips have revealed.

Ho! Christian, arise from the dust of the grave!
Thy Saviour is near thee to greet and to save.
The trump of Jehovah hath sounded on High
To lead thee to glory.—Thy Saviour is nigh.

MORNING HYMN.

Arise! arise! and sing
'Neath the sun's first golden rays;
Let Heaven's broad arches ring
With the accents of thy praise.

That hymn on Seraph's wings
Will soar beyond the sky,
And reach the King of Kings
Enthroned in realms on high.

And He will give thee light,
Pure beams of Heavenly Love,
To conquer in the fight
And find thy home above,

Where myriad voices sound
The triumphs of the Lord,
Where God on holy ground
For ever sheathes His sword.

Yea, by the crystal sea
All tears are wiped away,
And life's dark sorrows flee
In that Eternal day.

Awake,—awake,—and sing!
Oh! join the Angelic throng,
Till Heaven's broad arches ring
With the echoes of thy song

CHRISTMAS HYMN.

Hosanna! This day the Messiah was born.
Bow the knee to thy God in the blush of the morn!
Break forth into shouts as the sun gilds the sky,
For the glory of God sheds its rays from on high!
Hallelujah!

The star that the shepherds saw gleaming above
Was the beacon of mercy, the token of love;
Its soft beams are ever to shine in thy breast
And illumine thy path to the home of the blest.
Hallelujah!

That star was God's banner unfurl'd in the sky,
Far above in the heavens it glitters on high;

Beneath it, O Christian, enlist for the strife;
Make ready thine arms for the battle of life!
Hallelujah!

The guerdon is glory, a fadeless renown,
A mansion in heaven, a kingdom, a crown.—
Then pray to the Saviour to give thee to-day
The sword of the Spirit that conquers for aye!
Hallelujah!

Bow down to thy God in the blush of the morn;
Remember, this day the Messiah was born;
Break forth into shouts as the sun gilds the sky,
For the glory of God is proclaimed from on High!
Hallelujah!

TRANSLATIONS.

AMYNTAS.

The Prologue and Act I. Scene I.

From the Italian of Tasso.

THE PROLOGUE.

Cupid in a Shepherd's dress.

WHO would believe that in a mortal shape,
And 'neath the cover of this shepherd's dress,
A God were hid? And not, forsooth, some God
Of Sylvan race,—one of the lesser Gods,
But the most potent 'mong great Deities;
Who oft doth sever from the grasp of Mars
The ensanguined sword,—and from Neptune, (him
Who shakes the Earth,) his mighty trident wrests,
Ay! and th' eternal bolts from highest Jove.
With such a mien, and such a garb, in truth,

Venus, my mother, would not quickly mark
That I am Cupid, and her very son.
From her, my mother, I am forced to flee
And to conceal myself; since 'tis her wish
That I myself, mine arrows too, should bend
To her will. Ay! and more: with feminine
And vain ambition, she restricts mine aims
Alone to courts, to sceptres, and to crowns.
She doth insist mine acts be centred there;
And to my band of ministering aids,
My lesser brothers, solely licence gives
To dwell in forests, and to turn their arms
'Gainst rustic breasts. And I, who am no child
(Tho' childlike both in lineaments and acts),
As best it suits me choose to shape my course;
For Fate on *me*, and not on *her*, bestowed
The torch omnipotent and golden bow.

Yet oft I seek concealment, and do flee,
Not her control,—none hath she,—but her prayers,
That have great force when hard a mother pleads,
And refuge find amid the woods, and 'neath
The roofs of humble folk. But she pursues,—
Pledging to those, who should my person yield,
Either sweet kisses or some gift more prized;
As if I could not give as good exchange,—
Whether sweet kisses or some gift more prized,—
To silent tongues and those who keep me hid.
I hold *this* true, at least: dearest will be
My kisses ever unto youthful maids
(If I, Love's self, be in love-matters versed).
Hence Venus oft doth search for me in vain;
For they, not wishing I should be revealed,
Their counsel keep. And better to be veiled,
That she should know me by no outward signs,

I have abandoned quiver, bow, and wings.
Unarmed, withal, I have not hither come,
For this seeming wand is in truth my torch
(Thus I transformed it), and it breathes throughout
Flames that are hid from sight; and this my dart
(Although bereft of any point of gold),
Tempered by hand divine, doth love beget
Where'er it strikes. To-day I shall with this
Cause a deep wound, beyond all healing art,
In the flint breast of the most cruel Nymph
That ever followed in Diana's train.
Nor shall the wound be of less grievous kind
To Silvia (thus that mountain-nymph is called)
Than was the one that years long since gone by
Full in Amyntas' tender heart I dealt,
When he, a youth, and she, as young in years,
Followed the chase and mingled in the sports.

And that my thrust may deeper pierce her breast,
I shall await until compassion thaws
The ice of adamant girt round her heart
By Virtue's rigour and a virgin's pride;
And there shall strike where most the blow will tell.
That this good work to my great gain be done,
I shall set forth and mix in yonder crowd
Of shepherds revelling and with garlands crowned,
That now comes hither, where on holidays
It hath its pastimes; and, as I shall pass
For one among it, in this self-same place,
This very spot, I shall let fly my dart,
That mortal eye will have no power to see.
These woods to-day shall hear the theme of love
Broached in new guise. And it will then be plain
That my Divinity itself is here,
And acts not through its ministering aids.

I shall then breathe into rude, savage breasts
Nobility of feeling; sweeter make
Their language sound; for be where'er I may,
'Mid shepherds or 'mid heroes, I am Love;
And all my subjects' inequalities
I equalize, as best it pleaseth me,—
My greatest miracle,—my glory, this:
To make coarse reed yield sound of sweetest lyre;
And, if my mother, wroth to see me stray
Amid the woods, be ignorant of this,
'Tis *she* that's blind, in truth, not I myself,
Whom the blind vulgar call in error blind.

ACT I. SCENE I.

DAPHNE, SILVIA.

Daphne. Would'st thou then, Silvia, this desire
nurse,
To spend the spring-tide of thy tender youth
Far from the joys that Venus doth bestow?
Nor the dear name of Mother ever hear?
Nor see around thee children sweetly sport?
I do conjure thee, from thy purpose turn;
O foolish maiden, turn from it I pray.

Silvia. Let others court all those delights of love,
If in that love, indeed, delight there be;
This life doth suit me, and my pastime this:
My bow and arrows with due care to tend,
To track wild beasts that from me flee, to slay

The strong in combat; and, if then, perchance,
My quiver lack no shaft, nor fail the woods
To yield me prey, no lack of joys I dread.

Daphne. Insipid joys are these, in very truth,—
Insipid life too; if it pleaseth thee
'Tis that the other life thou hast not proved.
So the first mortal dwellers on this earth
(As yet in its infant simplicity)
Took for sweet beverage and delicious food
Water and acorns; and now both are held
As food and drink of animals alone,
Since we have learnt the use of corn and grapes.
Perhaps if thou shouldst taste but only once
A thousandth part of all those great delights
A loving heart doth feel when loved in turn,
With deep regret and sighing thou wouldst say:
"For ever lost is all that length of time

"Which was not wholly unto loving given.
"O years of life for ever passed away!
"How many widowed nights have been my lot,—
"How many days of solitary state
"Have I consumed in vain, and reaped no fruits,—
"Days that could all in loving have been spent,
"That oftener practised ever sweeter seems!"
O foolish maiden! from thy purpose turn,
For late repentance is of no avail.

Silvia. When I shall say, with penitence and sighs,
Those words by thee imagined and adorned
After thy liking, rivers shall return
Unto their sources; and the wolves shall flee
From lambs, and hounds by timid hares be chased;
The sea by bears, the Alp by dolphins sought.

Daphne. Full well I know that childish waywardness;
Such as thou art, I was; my form like thine;

Like thine my face ; my tresses quite as fair ;
And as vermilion as thy lips were mine ;
With whiteness as on thine the rose was mixed
On dimpled cheeks as soft. My chief delights
(Well I perceive their utter folly now)
Were spreading nets and laying bird-lime down,
Upon a flint well sharpening my dart,
Marking the trail or spying out the lair
Of beasts of prey ; and, if at times like these
I saw myself by eager lover watched,
Mine eyes were lowered to the ground, for wild
And rustic, full of bashful wrath was I.
Unwelcome to me was my beauty e'en,
A source of pain the more I seemed to please,
As if the fault were mine, and mine the shame
And insult, to be wished for, watched and loved.
But what effects not time? Or fails to do

By services, by merits, and by prayers,
A lover faithful and importunate?
That I was conquered, I confess to thee;
The victor's arms were these: humility,
With patience, tears and sighs, and mercy sought.
The shades of one brief night then showed me all
A thousand days' long course and light had failed
To show. I blamed myself and my so blind
Simplicity; and 'mid my sighs, I said:
"Here is thy horn, O Cynthia, here thy bow;—
"For I resign thy shafts,—renounce thy life."—
Thus do I hope that thy Amyntas may
This, thy rude nature, some day learn to tame,
And melt thy heart of iron and of flint.
Is he not comely then? Loves he not thee?
Or is it then that others love him not?
Or doth he change to suit another's love,

Or for the hatred that thou showest him ?
Is it in birth that he doth yield to thee ?
If Cidippus begot thee, he whose sire
Was God of this our noble river here,
Amyntas is Silvanus' son, to whom
Was father, the great God of shepherds, Pan.
Not less than thou is Amaryllis fair
(If on thy features thou dost ever gaze
Within the mirror of some fountain), yet
He doth despise all her sweet flatteries,
And still submits to thy disdainfulness
And sore vexations. But imagine now
(God grant that such a notion may be vain)
That he, despised by thee, should in the end
Love her who now so fondly doats on him :
What would'st thou feel ? and with what eyes be-
hold

Him by another owned? and happy made
In other arms, with scornful smiles for thee?

Silvia. What best doth please him, let Amyntas do
With himself and with his loves; nought care I:
So mine he be not, be he whose he will.
But mine he cannot be, if I wish not;
Nor even were he mine, would I be his.

Daphne. Whence, then, is born thy hatred?

Silvia. Of his love.

Daphne. Oh! gracious sire of a cruel son!
But when, I pray, were gentle lambs e'er born
Of tigers, or did lovely swans bear crows?
Me, or thyself, thou dost deceive.

Silvia. I hate
His love which mine own modesty doth hate;
I loved him while he only sought of me
What I desired.

Daphne. Thou did'st desire but harm
For thine own self. And he desires for thee
What he doth most desire for himself.

Silvia. Daphne, be still, or speak of other things
If thou seek'st answers.

Daphne. Oh! what wilful ways,
And what a wayward maid art thou! Reply
At least to *this*: Suppose another's love
Were given thee, would'st thou receive it thus?

Silvia. In self-same guise would I each one receive
Who should lay snares for my virginity.
Whom you a lover, I a foe do call.

Daphne. Think'st thou the ram, then, to the ewe a foe?
Or 'twixt the bull and heifer there's a feud?
The dove at war with its own faithful mate?
Or holdest thou this season sweet of Spring

A time of wrath and enmity? which now
Makes the heart joyful, and with smiling face
Once more enjoins the world—all animals—
All men and women to give way to love.
What! seest thou not how all created things
Are now enamoured, and their love how full
Of joy and health? Behold that turtle-dove
That with sweet murmurs and with flattering ways
Its gentle mate caresses. Hear awhile
That nightingale that now, from branch to branch,
Wanders, while singing thus: "I love, I love."
And (if thou know'st it not) the snake e'en sheathes
Its poisoned fang, and hastes to join its love.
Why! tigers, and the lion, for all his pride,
Succumb to love. And thou, shalt *thou* alone,
O haughty maid! more than e'en beasts of prey,
Deny love harbour in thy breast? But why

Discourse of lions, tigers, crawling snakes,
That all with feeling are endued? Why! e'en
The trees do love. With what affection, mark,
And with how many oft-repeated clasps,
Unto its spouse the vine doth closely cling!
The fir a fir, the pine a pine doth love;
Each ash for ash, each willow for its mate,
Each beech for beech doth ever burn and sigh.
And yonder oak, that seems so rough and wild,
Doth e'en itself experience all the power
Of amorous fire. And did'st thou but possess
The soul and sense of love within thee, then
Its silent sighs thou well would'st understand.
Is it thy wish to be of less account
Than e'en the plants, by thus avoiding love?
I do conjure thee from thy purpose turn.
Thou senseless maiden, turn from it, I say!

Silvia. Go to! when sighs from plants I hear, why then
I'll be content to fall in love at once.

Daphne. My faithful counsels dost thou then deride,
And mock my reasonings thus? O thou, to love
Both deaf and foolish! But go on, go on!
A day will come when thou shalt feel remorse
That they were scouted. Not alone, I say,
That all the fountains thou shalt flee, where now
Oft thou dost mirror thee with great delight,
Perchance; but thou shalt flee those fountains then
Solely for fear lest thou should'st see thyself
Deformed and ugly; that will be thy meed.
Nor do I presage thee but this alone;
Though great the ill, 'tis but a common ill.
For dost thou not recall what, two days past,
Elpinus, sage Elpinus, did recount
To fair Lycoris? She, who with her eyes

Wrought on Elpinus that which he, in sooth,
Through Song's great pow'r ought to have worked
on *her*
(Could love alway what *ought to be* command).
And he, Elpinus, then related thus
(Battus and Thyrsis being present, both
Great masters, truly, in the art of love):
That in Aurora's cave, where o'er the mouth
'Tis writ: "Away! away! all ye profane"—
He did relate, I say,—what he had learnt
From him who grandly sang of arms and love,
And dying, did bequeath to him his flute,—
That a black pit in Tartarus is found
Where smoke of noxious odour doth arise
From the sad furnaces of Acheron;
And punished there for everlasting time,
In torments dire of darkness and of tears,

All loveless and ungrateful women pine.
Expect that there a place shall be prepared
To give reception to thy nature fierce.
'Tis fit indeed, that smoke should ever draw
Tears from those eyes, that pity never drew.
Pursue thy bent, pursue it, wilful maid!

Silvia. What did Lycoris, then? How answered she?

Daphne. Thou carest not what thine own conduct is;
Yet would'st thou know what others' acts may be.
She with her eyes did answer him.

Silvia. But how
Can such reply with eyes alone be made?

Daphne. Her eyes replied with a sweet smile, unto
Elpinus turned: "Both heart and we are thine.
"Thou can'st not more demand; nor e'en can she
"Give more to thee. This should alone suffice

"To lover chaste, and be his sole reward,—
"If he but hold the eyes to be as true
"As they are fair, and give them fullest faith."

Silvia. And why not believe them?

Daphne. Know'st thou not, then,
What Thyrsis wrote, when, to his love a prey,
He wandered through the forests, quite distraught,
So that to pity and to laughter both
The gentle nymphs and shepherds were constrained?
Nor did he write what should to laughter move,
Though he might do what laughter should deserve.
He wrote his verses on a thousand trees;
With these they grew, and thus I read on one:
"*Ye mirrors of the heart, false, faithless lights!*
"*Well do I recognise all your deceits;*
"*But where's my gain, if Love bar my escape?*"

Silvia. In converse here, I let the time slip by,

Nor bear in mind that 'tis prescribed to-day
To hold the chase within the ilex-wood.
Now, if it please thee, wait until such time
As I do quit me, in the 'customed fount,
Of heat and dust that yesterday I gained,
As in the hunt a nimble fawn I chased,
Reached it at last, and slew it.

Daphne. I will wait,—
And, in the fount, perchance, I too shall bathe;
But first I would unto my home repair,
For 'tis not late, as it doth seem to be.
Wait at thy dwelling till I come to thee,
And meanwhile, think on what's more weighty still
Than chase or fount. If thou be ignorant,
Believe 'tis so,—and in the wise put faith.

THE DIVER.

(FROM THE GERMAN OF SCHILLER.)

" Who dares, be he Knight or Squire bold,
" To dive where the waters hiss?
" I throw down e'en now a goblet of gold;—
" 'Tis lost in that dark abyss.
" He who once more that goblet has shown,
" May keep the prize and call it his own."

Thus spake the King as the cup he made fly
Far into the depths below,
From where a great rock rises bluff and high,
And the sea's broad waters flow.
" Who is so bold, I say once more,
" As to dive and bring that cup ashore?"

And the Knights and Squires round the Monarch grouped
Were mute, though they heard him speak;
Where the wild billows raged and surged they stooped,
And none dared the goblet seek.
For the third time now the King spake so:
" Is there no one who dares to dive below?"

And, as before, not a tongue gives sound,—
But a youth, of gentle birth and bold,
Steps from among the Squires around,
Freed from his mantle and girdle's fold;
And all the men and women there
With wonder gaze on the youth so fair.

And as he reaches that tall rock's height,
He scans the abyss below,

And the billows around in maddened flight,
The whirlpool hemming the waters' flow,
As, with the thunder's distant roar,
On the sea's dark bosom in foam they pour.

And they seethe and they boil, and they heave and
they hiss,
As when the wild waters are mingled with fire,
And the steam-mantled spray seems the Heavens to
kiss,
While wave follows wave to roll on with new ire.
Of strength or of volume lost in scorn,
As if to the sea a new sea were born.

At length that fury fierce is spent,
And darkly against the snow-white foam
Yawns in the rock a huge wide rent,
Deep as if leading to Satan's home ;

While many a mighty, heaving wave
Hurled in the crater finds its grave.

Then, e'er the breakers returned once more,
The youth to his Maker muttered a prayer;—
A cry of alarm was heard from the shore;
The whirlpool had swept him away to its lair,—
And mysteriously over the swimmer bold,
Now lost in their jaws, the billows rolled.

A silence then reigned o'er the waters' abyss,
While below sounds of waves surging fell;
Quivered words on all lips, and their import was
this:
"Noble-hearted young hero, farewell!"
More hollow the echoes that howl in the Deep,
And fear and suspense all in agony keep.

And they cried: "Should'st thou throw, King, thy
diadem fair
"In the depths, and say: he, who can bring it to me,
"O'er this realm shall be King and that diadem wear,
"No such guerdon as this should we wish for from
thee.
"For all that those hoarse, roaring waters conceal
"No joy-breathing soul on this earth can reveal."—

"Full many a ship, to the vortex a prey,
"On a sudden has sunk far below the dark wave,
"Leaving mast and keel shattered—sole remnants
that lay
"On the sea's bosom, spared from th' insatiable
grave."—
And clearer and clearer, as storms break on shore,
Draws the sound ever nearer of billows that roar.

And they seethe and they boil, and they heave and
they hiss,
As when the wild waters are mingled with fire,
And the steam-mantled spray seems the Heavens to
kiss,
While wave follows wave to roll on with new ire.
And, with the loud thunders' far echoing roar,
O'er ocean's dark breast with blind fury they pour.

And lo! from that dark, troubled breast of the deep,
The waves rise like swans in a mantle of snow,
While an arm and a neck, gleaming white, onward
sweep,
And all the trained strength of a keen swimmer
show.
'Tis he!—and with joy he waves high in his left
The goblet of gold from the deep billows reft.

A long breath he drew,—and a deep breath he drew,
And saluted the heavenly light ;—
From neighbour to neighbour the good tidings flew
" He's saved ! yes, he lives ! He's in sight !
" From the grave, from the storm-beaten caves of the
sea,
" From destruction, the hero his soul has set free ! "

He comes,—and around him shouts jubilant ring ;
At the feet of the Monarch he falls,
And kneeling presents the gold cup to the King,
Who now to his fair daughter calls ;
While she fills up with wine the bright goblet of gold,
The youth to the Monarch this stirring tale told :

" Long life to the King ! Well may mortals be glad
" Who breathe in the day's rosy light !—

"In the Deep all is terrible, bitter and sad;
"No mortals should pray to the Gods for a sight
"Of all that in mercy they veil from their eyes,
"And shroud in the vesture of night's darkest skies.

"With the speed of the lightning, waves swept me
below;
"In a rocky abyss I was hurled in their flight
"Against a broad stream where the swift waters flow;
"And seized by two currents' impetuous might,
"Like a whirlpool, in dizzy wide circles was caught,
"And against their wild fury I helplessly fought.

"God, to whom for support I then turned me again,
"In my sore and most terrible need,
"Showed a high rocky ledge rising out of the main;
"I grasped it;—from death I was freed.

" And there hung the goblet, on coral reef bound,
" Else in depths it had sunk that no lead can e'er
sound.

" The fathomless waters I saw far below
" 'Mid the thick, purple darkness of night,
" And,—although by the ear not a mortal could know
" They were present,—the eye with affright
" Saw huge lizards and dragons crawl slowly, or
bound
" In that fearful abyss that was yawning around.

" Swarming medley of monsters, of ebony hue,
" Coiled in clusters, and ghastly, they gape,—
" The Ray, thorny-finned,—the Sea-Wolf came in
view,
" The Hammer-fish, hideous in shape;

" And Ocean's Hyæna, the Shark, lay beneath,
" And threat'ningly showed me his cruel, sharp teeth.

" There I clung,—and my spirit with dread was
pursued,
" For no human aid could be near,—
" 'Mid those spectres, *I* only with feeling endued,
" Alone in that solitude drear,—
" Far below the sweet music of man's friendly tongue,
" 'Mid the horrible shapes of that mournful wild,
flung.

" With these thoughts I shuddered,—when, crawling,
drew near
" A monster, its hundred joints moving ;
" It strove to snap at me,—a prey to wild fear,
" My grasp from the coral branch losing,

"I was caught by the flood,—yet it came but to
save,—
"For it bore me above on the breast of the wave."—

At the story he heard, marvelled greatly the King,
And he said: "Youth, the goblet is thine;
"'Tis my pleasure, moreover, to give thee this ring
"Set with gems from the most precious mine,
"If thou once more attempt to bring tidings to me
"Of the things to be seen in the depths of the sea."

His daughter had listened, and moved by the tale,
Spoke in words to persuasive tones wed:
"Cease, O Father, from sports that such horrors entail!
"He has done what all other men dread.
"If thou failest the lust of thy hard heart to tame,
"Let these Knights who stand round put the Squire
to shame."—

But swiftly the King seized the goblet of gold,
In the whirlpool he hurled it with might;
"Bring it up from the depths where the waters have
rolled!
"Then," he said, "thou shalt be my best knight."
"And to-day shalt thou call my sweet daughter thy
bride,
"Who with pity's soft voice pleads thy cause by my
side."

Then the youth's soul was fired by Heavenly Power,
From his bright eyes flashed valour's own light,
As he saw the deep blush of that lovely, sweet
flower,
Saw her droop as if smitten with blight;
Strongly stirr'd, he resolved the high prize to obtain;—
For life or for death, he dashed into the main.—

True,—the breakers are heard,—true, they roll back
to land,
Announced by their thunders' loud roar;
True, with love's gaze the lady now watches the
strand,
And they come, all those waters, to shore;
And they rush on above, and they rush on below,—
But they bring back no diver as onward they flow.

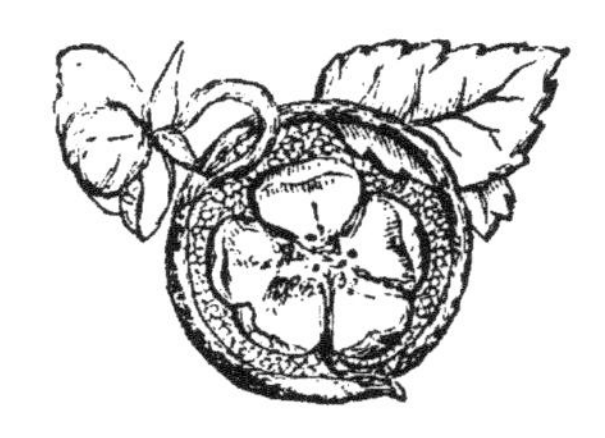

THE SWORD SONG.

FROM THE GERMAN OF KÖRNER.

Thou trusty brand at my left hand,
What means that sunny smile?
Those friendly rays, that meet my gaze,
With mirth each day beguile.
Hurrah!

"A noble Knight of many a fight
"Bears me; for him my joy.
"In Freedom born, by Freeman worn,
"My bliss hath no alloy."
Hurrah!

Yes, noble sword,—I pledge my word,—
I'm free, yet bound to thee,

As if a bride were by my side,
Or maid betrothed to me.
Hurrah!

"In woe or weal, this form of steel
"For aye shall be with thee.
"Oh! for a sign that thou art mine!
"When com'st thou, love, for me?"
Hurrah!

The trumpet's call proclaims to all
Our marriage morn is near;
When cannons roar, when flows the gore,
I'll come for thee, my dear.
Hurrah!

"Oh! happy kiss of endless bliss!
"I long to call thee mine.

"Oh! take thy bride unto thy side,
"Her maiden heart is thine."
Hurrah!

Why rings my steel a stirring peal
Within its mailèd sheath,
Like joyful sound of battleground
Where warriors win their wreath?
Hurrah!

"Would'st know, love, why I raise that cry?
"'Tis for the bloody fight;
"For this I long, for this I'm strong,
"For this I'm keen and bright."
Hurrah!

Nay, do not roam beyond thy home
To seek the light above;

There thou must stay, nor turn away
Until I come, my love!

Hurrah!

"Oh! leave me not in this lone spot,
"Far from those flowery plains,
"So tinged with glows of blood-red rose
"Where death in beauty reigns."

Hurrah!

Leap from thy sheath! no victor's wreath
Was ever prized as thou;
Come forth, my blade! for with thine aid
Our country's foes must bow.

Hurrah!

"What joy for me to feel I'm free!
"Ho! for the bridal meal!

" Lit by the ray of brilliant day,
" How brightly shines the steel ! "
Hurrah !

Rise, as of old, ye warriors bold !
Erect each Teuton crest !
Are your hearts cold ? then quickly fold
The loved one to your breast.
Hurrah !

In blushing pride at our left side
She glances furtively,
Till on the right, in all men's sight,
Her bridal place shall be.
Hurrah !

Then fondly seal those lips of steel,
Aye ! press her to thy side ;

And curs'd be he, whoe'er he be,
Who dares desert his bride!
Hurrah!

Now let her sing,—and loudly ring
Unfettered at our side;
Behold the dawn, the marriage morn!
Hurrah! thou iron-bride!
Hurrah!

THE FOUNTAIN.

FROM THE GERMAN OF KÖRNER.

Bold as youth that knows no fear
Watch the silvery waters rise,
Like to crystal, pure and clear,
Springing upward to the skies.
    Ever higher, ever higher,
    Sparkling in the sun's strong fire,
    Scarce to melt in spray on high,
    E'er once more they heav'nward fly.

Mark the pure, soft light of day
Part in countless crystal gleams,
And each brilliant iris-ray
Weave that misty veil of beams.

Thus my aspirations wing
Thro' the clouds to Heaven's realm,
Thus a thousand wishes spring
And in flames my heart o'erwhelm.

But as yonder rainbow beams
Join in *one* pure ray of light,
So my earthly hopes and dreams
Centre round *one* beacon bright.
And my yearning heart o'erflowing
Sinks in worship at Love's throne,
Thrills with mystic, dim foreknowing,
Like a dream of worlds unknown.

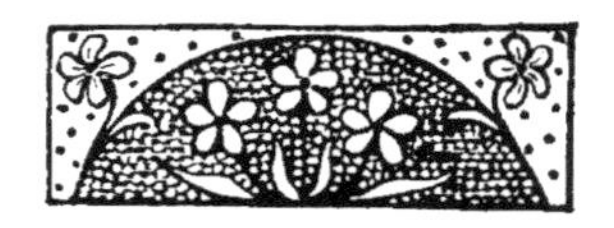

LÜTZOW'S WILD CHACE.

(LEIPZIG, *24th April* 1813.)

FROM THE GERMAN OF KÖRNER.

What gleams from yon wood in the sunshine around?
Ever nearer I hear a sound roll;
And dark, serried masses fast cover the ground,
While madly the shrill notes of bugles resound,
That with dread and dismay fill the soul.
If you ask those black comrades who ride such a pace,
They'll tell you 'tis Lützow's wild, dare-devil chace.

Who are those who rush swiftly up yon wooded height,
And from hill-side to hill-side o'erflow?
And now they lie hid in the shades of the night,

Hurrahs loud are shouted,—wing bullets their flight,
And the legions of France are laid low.
If you ask those black hunters who ride such a pace,
They'll tell you 'tis Lützow's wild, dare-devil chace.

Safe the ruffians bethought them, where Rhine's waters
roar,
And where brightly the grapes ever glow,
But storm-like the horsemen rushed,—onward they
bore,
And through the deep waters with strong arms they
tore,
Till they sprang on the land of the foe.
If you ask those black swimmers who swim such a pace,
They'll tell you 'tis Lützow's wild, dare-devil chace.

Who are they in the valley who war with such might,
Swords clashing 'mid battle's deep roar?

They are warriors bold, who have fought the good
fight,
And the altars of Freedom are glowing with light,
And blaze with the fierce flames of gore.
If you ask those black riders who ride such a pace,
They'll tell you 'tis Lützow's wild, dare-devil chace.

Who are they whose last sigh breathes adieu to the
light,
Couched 'mid foes who so plaintively moan?—
Death's quivering hand is fast veiling their sight,
Yet these true hearts are firm, and his terrors they
slight,
For free is the country they own!
Ask those black, stricken heroes who rode such a
pace,
They'll tell you 'twas Lützow's wild, dare-devil chace.

Yes ! that wild, headlong chace, and that wild, German
chace!
'Twas for tyrant's and murderer's breath !
Then ye who us love, let no tears dew your face,
For our country is free ;—night to morning gives place ;
Though Freedom was conquered through Death !
And for ever be told to all sons of our race,
The tale of brave Lützow's wild, dare-devil chace !

ILSANES.

FROM THE GERMAN OF MATHAY.

Within her garden of roses, the fair and youthful
Queen
Chriemhilde stands; she watches where the gate of
Worms is seen;
For all the knights within the realm are summoned
far and wide
At her behest, to join the joust, and hither swift they
ride!
And towards her spouse, King Dieterich, turns fair
Chriemhilde now,
While stroking back the silvery locks from off his
lofty brow,
Her dewy lips of roseate hue with warmest kisses seek

The Monarch's lips, and these the words that tenderly they speak:
"Not long ago I boasted thus,—by soul and body swore,
"No woman's spouse a greater name than mine for courage bore.
"My promise to redeem to-day, I called this knightly host.—
"Arise, thou mighty King, arise, make good thy Consort's boast!"
Then with deep wonder stricken, he looked up, that Monarch old,
Straight in Chriemhilde's eyes he gazed till she grew hot and cold;
And she her anxious fears to veil, on many a subject spoke,
But still the King kept watching her, nor once his silence broke.

Now thro' the painful stillness resounds this trumpet-
call:
"In armour bright, prepared to fight, the Knights
are gathered all!"
And soon Chriemhilde's trembling doubts to highest
spirits yield,
When near the lists she sees the King prepared to
take the field.
Chriemhilde hastes to join him there, and now before
he goes,
Her arm, as if in fond farewell, she softly round him
throws,
While secretly unfastening the gorget's outer clasp,
That linked it to the coat of mail with firm unbending
hasp!
As the grey-haired Monarch mounted (still sturdy he
appeared)

It seemed as if a tear-drop rolled adown his silvery
beard;
But whether tear of sorrow or of wrath none there
could glean,
For like iron, as his armour, his face by all was seen;
And as within the barriers now the King came into
sight,
With stealth approached Chriemhilde a youthful,
comely Knight:
"Count Staudenfuss of Rhineland!" he said. One
look alone
Sufficed to frame his question, and to make her
answer known.

The Tournament now opens; but the Monarch stays
as yet,
For on vanquishing the strongest his mind is firmly set.

Count Staudenfuss of Rhineland it was, who at the last
Victorious stood. The Monarch then at him defiance
cast.
With standing long outwearied, the King's impetuous
steed,
Impatient, stamped and pawed the ground, but on a
sudden freed,
Like cannon ball from heavy gun, with thunder's
crash he sped,
While sword struck sword with clashing sound, and
far the echo spread.
But neither yields. The King himself, a giant, hard
as steel,
Sits like a rock. His rival's steed is backward forced
to wheel.
But, at the second charge between these two con-
tending foes,

The Count more clearly sees the spot that no protection shows;
There in the neck with thrust of lance, the King he deeply gores,
Till from the death-wound fast the blood upon the arena pours.
As red, and ever redder, grows the Monarch's coat of mail,
So pale his noble face becomes, each moment still more pale;—
And falling from his charger now, the Knights and ladies fair
Surround his lifeless body; and not one spectator there
That does not vent his grief aloud,—save Chriemhilde, the Queen;
Quite motionless she stands; no tears in those bright eyes are seen.

"In truth 'twould ill beseem me now the spouse to
mourn, who fell
"By braver man in combat slain,—and what I promised—well!
"The victor shall obtain;" she said—"Count Staudenfuss, for this
"Receive from me, in knightly thanks, a garland and
a kiss!"—
And while as yet this trait'rous pair in fast embrace
are bound,
Outside the garden, echoes, like a horse's hoofs, resound!
Up comes a mounted herald, with a black armorial
shield
Where a salamander gloweth on a gold and crimson
field.
"Your pardon, Queen Chriemhilde, but a guest, right
strange 'tis true,

"This black shield's owner to these lists an entrance craves from you.
"He knows the prize, the highest 'tis, that this our earth can show,
"On *him*, this wondrous hero swears, that prize you shall bestow!"—
He hardly ceased, ere from the crowd full deep the murmurs grow,
As in the lists a monk appears with face as white as snow!
His steed was black, but saddle-less, his grey garb, woven hair;
A broad and shining sword he wears, his only weapon there;
From chin to breast a raven beard in waving motion flows,
In his sad eyes both grief is shown, and lust of combat glows!

"Well know'st thou me, Chriemhilde," he said, "Thou beauteous Queen,
"This day I woo thee, and I'll bend thy stubborn will, I ween;
"The kiss thou shalt bestow, that once thy lips refused to yield,
"For thou wert rich, and I possessed but this my sword and shield!
"Count Staudenfuss, I summon thee to God's decree for this,
"That thou a traitor's part hast played to win the wreath and kiss!"—
And now Chriemhilde trembles. Full well the Monk she knows,
And shame paints on her cheek the while her deepest tint of rose.
A greater dread of this Monk's speech than of his weapon bright

Feels Staudenfuss, and therefore now he girds him
for the fight.
And as he mounts his charger, men scarcely draw
their breath,
And as he bares his weapon, all round 'tis still as
death ;
As when about a scaffold, the silent crowd press near,
And on the hapless culprit fix their gaze, in cruel
fear
Lest of that dreadful moment's sight perchance they
should be reft,
When by the sword the victim's head from off the
trunk is cleft.
Thus was it when the herald sent forth his trumpet-
call.—
It sounds. The combat now begins, that seems so
strange to all ;

The Count in rigid armour; the Monk in garb of hair,
But well he knew how best to wield his bright broad
weapon there.
Down to the throat he split in twain proud Stauden-
fuss's head,
Thro' iron and thro' steel he cleft, and high the life-
blood sped,
Like to some mighty waterspout, and stained the
ploughed-up sands;
—The Monk stood still in silent prayer, with meekly
folded hands.—
The Knight falls from his charger. The men, and
women fair
Turn from his corse,—a secret dread seems slowly
creeping there
Throughout the awe-struck crowd. Alone Chriem-
hilde loudly weeps,

And from those beauteous eyes of hers full many a tear-drop leaps.
Said the Monk: "'Twould ill beseem thee thy lover dead to mourn,
"By braver man in combat slain,—and what thy lips have sworn
"To give the victor, must be mine! Quick! wreath and kiss for me,
"For back within the Convent walls, to-night I needs must be!"—
On this he tears the rose-wreath from off that woman fair,
And now her slender form he clasps with mighty pressure there,
With kisses holds her to his breast,—his arms so strong enfold
As tho' he ne'er would loose her;—she sank down dead and cold!

"With like sharp-edgèd sword the men,—the women with like kiss,
"Who holiest trust betray," he said, "so shamefully as this,—
"Chastises Monk Ilsanes,—and were it now decreed
"That I should die this hour,—I did a righteous deed!"
And when he thus had spoken, he exulting rode away.—
The Convent's mighty bell is heard, ere passes many a day,—
Weird tolling thro' the solemn chaunts; the sound each heart appals . . . .
'Tis for the Monk Ilsanes, built up, living, in its walls.

THE WATCH BY THE RHINE.

FROM THE GERMAN OF C. WILHELM.

Shouts deep as thunder wake the shore,
Like clash of arms and Ocean's roar,
To the Rhine! The Rhine! The German Rhine!
Who will watch where those waters shine?
Dear Fatherland, calm trust be thine:
True men are watching by the Rhine.

Those shouts the breasts of legions thrill,
All eyes with fiery flashes fill,
Swords of the noble, strong and brave,
The sacred landmarks guard and save.
Dear Fatherland, calm trust be thine:
True men are watching by the Rhine.

As the warrior scans the azure dome,
Whence heroes gaze from their sacred home,
"O Rhine!" he cries, "we ne'er shall part,
"Be ever German as my heart."
Dear Fatherland, calm trust be thine:
True men are watching by the Rhine.

While one red drop our veins still yield,
While one right arm the blade can wield,
By one hand still the ball be sped,
No foe thy sacred shores shall tread.
Dear Fatherland, calm trust be thine:
True men are watching by the Rhine!

The oath is sworn, fast flows the tide,
High on the breeze the banners ride.

To the Rhine! The Rhine! The German Rhine!
We *all* watch where those waters shine!
Dear Fatherland, calm trust be thine:
True men are watching by the Rhine!

THE SOLDIER'S PRAYER.

FROM THE GERMAN.

O Lord! Thou art my star by night,
My glorious sun by day,
My shield of Faith, my sole delight,
Where'er my footsteps stray.

Since Thou, O Lord! art ever near,
Can pilgrim-man have cause to fear?

Give to my arm the strength to wield
The sword for justice drawn;
Grant that to foes I ne'er may yield,
Of honour ne'er be shorn!

Lay bare the breast of ev'ry foe!
Oh! guide my hand,—direct my blow!

May ne'er my steed his footsteps miss
When yawns the chasm wide!
Send angels from Thy realms of bliss
My ways to watch and guide!

Be Thou my star,—my only stay,—
When o'er the desert lies my way!

Give me to scent Thy balmy breeze,
To feel Thy grateful shade,
When pale fatigue my limbs shall seize,
And sight and strength shall fade!

Close Thou mine eyes, and let me roam
O'er heav'nly realms, and find my home!

THE FOUNDING OF THE CONVENT OF LIMBURG.

FROM THE GERMAN OF ZÜLLIG.

'Neath the shadow of his lime trees, upon his Limburg
land,
Sat high-born Kaiser Conrad, of Franconia's princely
band.
More than all his other strongholds, this keep he
loved to see,
The old seat of his ancestors of knightly pedigree.

Thus oft to reach these halls from Worms his steed
he hotly pressed,
From many a mighty labour of pen and sword to
rest ;

Now crossing thro' the forests, now gazing from his
home,
O'er the fields of Worms and Speiergau his eyes were
wont to roam.

There sits he now and ponders; his eyes, tho' kindly,
gleam,
And secretly his bosom swells with many a pleasant
dream;
For glorious and more glorious still before him
visions rise
Of lineage old, and all wherein his kingdom's great-
ness lies.

From simple knight to feudal lord, and upwards then
to Count,
To Duke and now to Emperor, thus came his line to
mount.

Soon land on land, now held in fee, shall fall into his hand,
And soon his banner wave on high on Ocean's distant strand.

For strong shall be the Emperor; men "great" the realm shall hail;
Before the star of Germany soon many a star shall pale:
A short span more for Conrad! But should it not be so,
The second Conrad's realm full soon a Conrad third will know.

"Where halts my son?" the Monarch said, "with sport he must have met,
"To make him in the forest depths the lapse of time forget;

"Yet surely, e'er brief moments pass, the boy will
soon be here
"With triumph flushed, to shew to me the forest's
goodly cheer.

"On *him* may Germans rest their hopes! How bold
his glance around!
"How swiftly from him boar and bear deep in the
forest bound!
"How soon his mind has seized!—but hark! what
cry is that I hear?
"'Tis not a sound with joy to thrill, but evil news to
fear."—

Came a squire to the king and said: "We sorrow for
thy sake,
"Thy little son has fallen from the steep path by the
lake.

"Up the mountain he rode swiftly, and seeming nought to heed,
"But his courser swerved, and down the gorge then rushed at fullest speed."

Up ran another yet and said: "We sorrow for thy sake;
"Thy little son lies rigid in the chasm by the lake.
"We call,—he hears no longer; we list,—he breathes no more;
"And in his eyes the light, alas! has set for evermore."—

The Monarch wrung his hands and cried: "Alas! my son, my son!
"What use are now my crown and throne, and all these riches won?

"Away, ambition's schemes, away! Thou too, my house, away!
"No more I care to dwell in thee,—a Convent from to-day!"—

Unto the Abbot Boppo, then, t'wards Stabelo he rode,
And said: "I give thee this my house to be God's own Abode;
"May many Masses here be said, and henceforth thus be won
"God's Mercy for my darling child,—Alas! my son, my son!"

THE CRUCIFIX.

FROM THE FRENCH OF VICTOR HUGO.

Come, ye that weep, oh! come to Him,
For, lo! He weepeth too;
O ye that suffer, come to Him,
For He will comfort you!

Come, ye that faint and weary sigh,
For you His smile is shed;
He awaits the Pilgrim passing by;
To Him your steps be led!

Come, ye that weep and sorrow here,
For He will share your grief;
Come, ye that mourn, for He is near,
And hath for all relief!

LONDON:

KERBY AND ENDEAN, PRINTERS, ETC.,

OXFORD STREET.

CPSIA information can be obtained
at www.ICGtesting.com
Printed in the USA
BVHW041329010319
541545BV00021B/783/P